AN EXHIBITION ORGANIZED BY THE LOS ANGELES COUNTY MUSEUM OF ART
IN COOPERATION WITH THE MUSEUM'S CONTEMPORARY ART COUNCIL AND UNDER THE DIRECTION OF
JULES LANGSNER

LOS ANGELES COUNTY MUSEUM OF ART, LYTTON GALLERY, 1966

Observation Time — The Lovers, 1932—34
Oil
$39^3/_8 \times 98^1/_2''$
Private Collection

À L'HEURE DE L'OBSERVATOIRE ~ LES AMOUREUX

Lenders to the Exhibition

Mr. and Mrs. Raul Alvarez, New York
Michael Asher, Los Angeles
Mr. and Mrs. Edwin Bergman, Chicago
Mr. and Mrs. Michael Blankfort, Los Angeles
Mme. Simone Colinet, Paris
D. and J. de Menil, Houston
Leo W. Farland, New York
Mrs. Andrew P. Fuller, New York
Claude Hersaint, Paris
Joseph Hirshhorn, New York
Mr. and Mrs. Melvin Jacobs, New York
Louis F. Kannenstine, New York
Jacques Kaplan, New York
Mr. and Mrs. Thomas Kelly, New York
Mr. and Mrs. Herbert Kendall, Princeton
Mr. and Mrs. Harold Knapik, New York
Mr. and Mrs. Albert Lewin, New York
Mr. and Mrs. Man Ray, Paris
Mrs. Patricia Kane Matisse, New York
Dr. and Mrs. Daniel Mattis, Shappaqua, New York
Mr. and Mrs. Morton G. Neumann, Chicago
I. M. Pei, New York
Sir Roland and Lady Penrose, London
Mr. and Mrs. Gifford Phillips, Santa Monica
Mr. and Mrs. Frank Porter, Cleveland
Mr. and Mrs. Vincent Price, Los Angeles
Mr. and Mrs. Bernard Reis, New York
Frida and Hans Richter, Southbury, Connecticut
Mr. and Mrs. George Rosenthal, Cincinnati
Mr. and Mrs. David Savage, Princeton
Samuel Siegler, Teaneck, New Jersey

Mrs. Kate Steinitz, Los Angeles
Dr. and Mrs. Howard Taswell, Rochester, Minnesota
J. Daniel Weitzman, New York
Dr. and Mrs. Paul Wescher, Santa Monica
Richard S. Zeisler, New York

The Columbus Gallery of Fine Arts
The Solomon R. Guggenheim Museum, New York
Moderna Museet, Stockholm
The Museum of Modern Art, New York
North Carolina Museum of Art, Raleigh
Philadelphia Museum of Art
Princeton University Art Museum
The Tate Gallery, London
Whitney Museum of American Art, New York
Yale University Art Gallery, New Haven
Yale University Library, New Haven

Cordier & Ekstrom, Inc., New York
Galerie Diderot, Paris
Galerie Larcade, Paris
P. N. Matisse, Beverly Hills
Galleria Schwarz, Milan

Foreword and Acknowledgements

The satisfaction derived from arranging this exhibition has been two-fold: the chance to become acquainted with the full range of Man Ray's work and the attainment of a more insightful grasp of his view of existence. With reference to Man Ray, each of these facets illuminates the other. Something he said twenty-odd years ago regarding his efforts as an artist is germane: "This work cannot be considered experimental. The pursuit of pleasure, my guiding motive, is not a science. Or, as I have previously stated, the desire, not the necessity is the stimulant." One cannot enjoin the spectator by fiat to approach the works in the exhibition in the spirit in which they were created. Even so, it is suggested that the spectator do just that.

Herewith, my recognition of the invaluable assistance rendered by William and Noma Copley, New York, David and Naomi Savage, Princeton, New Jersey, Arne Ekstrom of Cordier and Ekstrom Gallery, New York, and Paul and Mary Wescher, Santa Monica, California. Above all, my gratitude to Man and Juliet Ray who gave unstintedly of their time, patience, hospitality and friendship.

The exhibition would not have been possible without the enthusiastic response to the idea by Richard F. Brown, formerly Director of the Museum and James Elliott, formerly Chief Curator. I must acknowledge my indebtedness to William Osmun who was most helpful, and to Maurice Tuchman who coordinated and supervised the preparation of the exhibition and the production of the catalog. Miss Virginia Ernst assisted Mr. Tuchman.   Jules Langsner

Table of Contents

Man Ray
Paris
1934

8

About Man Ray: An Introduction

Jules Langsner

Man Ray has been painter, sculptor, maker of collages and objects, architectural draughtsman, designer, printmaker, chess player, writer, photographer, pioneer of avant-garde film, inventor, recluse, wit, bon vivant, and intimate of many notable figures in the arts of our century. Despite the multiplicity of his interests, he has looked upon himself as an artist since the age of seven when he elected that vocation as his calling. The high caliber and astonishing range of works in this exhibition substantiate that early and insightful view of himself.

None of the designations favored by critics, reviewers, art historians, curators, educators, psychoanalysts and other compulsive classifiers of art and the human spirit fit this inventive, seminal and protean artist. "I don't know what is original or modern," he has said, "I just try to be myself." Having an original cast of mind, he became a significant originator. The classifiers are going to classify whether their classifications are meaningful or not. One result of their labors has been to make Man Ray known primarily as one of the founders and leading spirits of Dada and Surrealism, all too often neglecting to mention, however, that he was the only American artist to play a prominent role in the launching of those two far-reaching movements. The New York painter, William Copley, spoke for the Pop and Neo-Dada generation of the Sixties when he called Man Ray, quite accurately and properly, "The Dada of Us All." Such Dada objects as *New York 1920* (an olive jar stuffed with steel balls) and *Cadeau* of 1921 (the famous flat iron with a row of nails, points outward, down the middle of the working surface) might have been conceived at any time within the past half-dozen years. Their impact has not diminished. His contributions to Surrealism are equally distinguished. Such paintings as *Observatory Time — The Lovers* (1932–1937) and *Le Beau Temps* (1939) are among the masterworks of Surrealism. Other surrealist works by him anticipate certain aspects of Pop Art — for example, *The Fortune* of 1938, in which a billiard table with three balls scattered over the top stretches into vast space. The picture relates to Pop Art in the meticulous rendering of ordinary things unexpectedly isolated for our contemplation. With this significant difference, however: Man Ray's surrealist pictures are invested with enigma, while Pop Art avoids the poetic and mysterious aspects of the commonplace.

Man Ray's contributions to Dada and Surrealism comprise a very large proportion of works in the exhibition, but there are many other arrows in his quiver. His varied achievements as an artist cannot be encapsulated within a couple of designations. Following the 1913 Armory Show in New York, an enlarging experience for him, as for other budding modernists of his generation, he became one of the pioneers of abstract art in America. Starting from a Cézanne phase, as in *The Village* of 1913, he evolved a highly personal Cubism, as in the tubular figures and horses of *A. D. MCMXIV* painted the next year, and in 1916 he ventured into Abstraction in such works as *The Rope Dancer Accompanies Herself with Her Shadows.* The *Rope Dancer* (along with certain other works between 1916 and 1920) parallel current efforts to interlock flat colorforms on the surface plane. As for the recent interest in giving paintings and painted sculpture a high-gloss, machine-like finish, Man Ray was involved with a similar intention in 1918 and 1919. Such works as the 1919 *Admiration of the Orchestrelle for the Cinematograph,* rendered entirely with airbrush, were conceived with the intention of giving forms a machined appearance.

For several decades Man Ray has followed the impulse of the moment wherever it has led him. He believes that "Art simply varies in its sources of inspiration and in its modes of execution. It can vary within one man, depending on his curiosity and on his sense of freedom ... The real experiment is in proportion to the desire to discover and enjoy, and this desire alone can be the only measure of the painter's value to the rest of society." Following the impulse of the moment, Man Ray may turn from painting to sculpture or collage or the making of an object or a rayograph or to the creation of works that fit no conventional designation. Is the *Lampshade* an object or a mobile? First conceived in 1919 of paper from a lamp, it was twisted into a spiral and suspended from the ceiling, rotating slowly as if imbued with a life of its own. What about *The Orator* of 1935, both painting and object? Or *Talking Picture* of 1954, a work incorporating a loudspeaker that, properly installed, is wired to a radio-phonograph? During recent years Man Ray has fashioned works listed as 'collages' in the catalog. In such string collages of 1965 as *Inquietude* and *The Necklace*, string projects into forward space, adding the advance and negative openings of relief to the pictures. In these, as well as in numerous other works in the show, Man Ray erased boundaries separating one medium from another. Unconcerned with the properties said to be intrinsic to this or that medium, he is among the first boundary-hoppers in twentieth century art.

Not only has Man Ray hopped boundaries separating established media, he has been among the handful of inventors of viable new art forms such as the rayograph (considered later in this introduction) and the 'object,' a new kind of visual entity he originated with his friend Marcel Duchamp. The object as work of art consists of ordinary artifacts which, pried loose from their usual setting and by their placement together, disclose hitherto unseen esthetic and psychological properties. The esthetic attributes of ordinary artifacts, in the sense of good design, had long been appreciated. What had not been perceived were the intrinsically formal properties of artifacts apart from their function and (equally important) the psychological overtones such artifacts might convey if viewed as works of art. The incorporation of ordinary artifacts in collage preceded the object. In collage, however, ordinary things are incorporated as part and parcel of a pictorial conception. In the object, artifacts (usually

Self Portrait, 1964 replica of 1916 original
Mixed media object
28 x 19"
Collection Mr. and Mrs. Man Ray, Paris

in their original state) are, themselves, the imagery offered for our perception. The intuitive eye of the artist transforms artifacts (as such) into a mode of imagery. Man Ray's *Smoking Device*, an object of 1959, for example, combines a pipe rack, some marbles, and a piece of rubber tubing. Nothing more, yet the startling strangeness and relationships of this grouping involves the spectator in a form of art experience.

The object owes its beginnings (in part) to the verbal imagery of the poet, Isadore Ducasse, who called himself the Comte de Lautréamont. In *Les Chants des Maldodor*, published in 1874, Lautréamont introduced such imagery as "... the chance encounter on a dissecting table of a sewing machine and an umbrella." This evocative and unexpected conjunction of everyday objects was to make Lautréamont one of the

patron saints of Surrealism. But Man Ray had been an admirer of Lautréamont long before the advent of Surrealism in 1924. His photograph of 1920, *The Enigma of Isadore Ducasse*, presents a haunting image of something that is itself an object, a bulging cloth tied down by ropes. No one but the artist knows what is under that disturbingly bulging cloth. It must forever remain undecipherable. It was Man Ray's tribute to the precocious (now shrouded in mystery) Comte de Lautréamont.

Man Ray never has adhered long to any stylistic direction. Indeed, he frequently has shifted back and forth between various attitudes to the image. Finding the date of one of his efforts may be interesting for one reason or another, but it is not necessarily illuminating information. The critic or art historian bent on tracing Man Ray's development, in the sense of some sort of

The Enigma of Isadore Ducasse, 1920
Mixed media object
Photograph by Man Ray
(destroyed)

11

progression, is bound to be, not only frustrated, but defeated. In this regard, there is the story he is fond of telling of his painting, *Rue Férou*, a 1952 picture of the little street off the Place St. Sulpice in Paris where he lives with his wife. The painting upset a friend who was visiting the studio. "Why did you do a thing like that? It's so realistic," the friend demanded to know. Characteristically, the artist replied, "Because I wasn't supposed to." Moreover, Man Ray always has felt free to restate a work of years before in a manner close in spirit to the original effort, or else resume an idea he may have put aside long ago, an idea that perhaps belongs to some earlier phase of his career.

Man Ray, in his capacity as artist, values to the highest degree his autonomy, his freedom to pursue his work in whatever way happens to interest him at the time. So far as he is concerned, such attributes as consistency, advance, progress, development, stylistic identity obstruct his total freedom to go his own way, wherever it may lead. Autonomy in the studio is of the utmost importance to him. Not long ago he stated his position with reference to his total freedom as an artist: "I like contradictions. We have never attained the infinite variety and contradictions that exist in nature. Tomorrow I shall contradict myself. That is one way I have of asserting my liberty, the real liberty which one does not find as a member of society." It is a declaration spoken in the essential spirit of Dada, a core aspect of Man Ray considered at some length later in this introduction.

There is another aspect of Man Ray's works that must be confronted: the seemingly cavalier attitude he sometimes has taken to the technical side of art. Numerous works in the exhibition demonstrate his craftsmanship. But craft, as such, does not interest him. Man Ray's conception of the technical side of art is crucial to full understanding of his approach to art experience. Therefore, it behooves the viewer to learn what he has to say about the matter. Twenty years ago, speaking of his own work, he wrote,

"In whatever form it is finally presented, by a drawing, by a painting, by a photograph, or by the object itself in its original materials and dimensions, it is designed to amuse, bewilder, annoy or to inspire reflection, but not to arouse admiration for any technical excellence usually sought for in

A.D. MCMXIV, 1914
Oil
36^1/$_2$ x 68^1/$_2$"
A. E. Gallatin Collection,
Philadelphia Museum of Art

works of art. The streets are full of admirable craftsmen, but so few practical dreamers."

For Man Ray, the execution of a work of art is significant in relation to the ideas that work embodies. Emphasis on technique may cloud ideas, or else conceal the artist's impoverishment of ideas. With regard to his own work, germinal ideas must be interesting in some way. By no means must such ideas be weighted with profound implications. They may be interesting if amusing, suggestive, provocative. Moreover, the idea for a work of art has to possess him. On this score he has said, "I never paint because I am a painter. I paint because I have an idea. I let the idea recur and recur; it has to haunt me until I *have* to put it down in concrete form." With all the forethought that may enter into the making of one of his works, Man Ray, true to his Dada and Surrealist inclinations, keeps himself wide open to the unforeseen, to chance, to accident, to the fortuitous.

Man Ray's penchant for giving many of his works witty titles disturbs some purist viewers and critics. Pure painting, painting that exists purely as such, is only of peripheral interest to him. The notion that words (or other "literary values") get in the way of the pure experience of art he considers just another "sacred cow." Highly literate and adept with words, the full flavor of many of his works can only be savored by fusing visual and verbal statements. Words often are an inseparable part of the visual imagery, just as a poem often is integral to Far Eastern painting. Something of value is lost in both instances when the words are severed from the visual entity. Sometimes, in the case of Man Ray, the verbal aspect involves a pun, or a play on words. This may present hazards to the spectator unfamiliar with French when the titles are in that language. Puns and plays on words often do not translate successfully. The object titled *Blue Bread* in English has entirely different connotations when presented with its original designation of *Pain Peint*. On the other hand, other titles,

such as that for the object, *Mirror to Die Laughing By,* do not lose by translation.

Man Ray is a wit with visual images and with words, and with both simultaneously. Moreover his wit is tinged with irony and, sometimes, with a drop of acid. Many Americans are ill-at-ease with irony, with his kind of playful quickness of intelligence. But Man Ray has lived in France for many years. In that country, ironic play with words, puns, double-entendre are admired and cultivated. That is one of the reasons he finds the intellectual milieu of Paris so congenial. Not surprisingly, the last word on the subject belongs to

Man Ray
Hollywood
1945
Photograph by Mrs. Man Ray

him — "If some of my works are ironical or joking that's because I am sure of myself." Not trying to be anything other than himself, there is no need for him to prove anything. Viewers uncomfortable with irony, the quip, the jest in works of art are advised to concentrate on other facets of Man Ray's work.

Man Ray the photographer, is no easier to pin down than Man Ray the artist. One suspects that he was bound, sooner or later, to take a crack at photography, considering his interest in all aspects of visual imagery and his disdain of the conventional division of art into fine and not-so-fine. When I asked him how he happened to get as involved with photography as he did around the close of the First World War, he gave me a different kind of answer altogether. The truth of the matter was, he explained, "I had to get money to paint. If I'd had the nerve, I'd have become a thief or a gangster, but since I didn't, I became a photographer." In this decision he was right. He emerged rapidly as one of the most noted photographers of the Twenties and Thirties, commanding handsome fees for portraits and fashion photography. Commissioned photography in no way diminished the quality or inventiveness of his work, whether for a fee or in an endeavor of his own determination. And as a photographer he was able to pursue his other work in the studio with the total freedom he finds essential to his well-being.

The invention of the rayograph was one of those chance discoveries familiar in science and technology. Without intending to do so, Man Ray left some objects on an unexposed negative. He discovered, to his surprise, when he developed the negative, that the objects left a white impression while the rest of the print remained black. This must have happened innumerable times before, but only someone prepared to take advantage of chance could have foreseen the possibilities for a new kind of photographic imagery produced entirely without the camera. That order of imagery occupies a domain somewhere between the black and white photograph and the black and white abstract print. The rayographs in the show reveal the scope and richness of this medium of expression. The reader interested in the artist's reflections on the rayograph should turn elsewhere in these pages to the statement on the subject by him.

Man Ray's films of the Twenties have exerted a continuing influence on avant-garde and commercial motion pictures. The three films of which prints have survived — *Emak Bakia, L'Etoile de mer* and *Les Mysteres du Chateau de dé* — extended the medium into previously unexplored kinds of imagery. The films, discussed in depth by Carl Belz in this catalog — were solely the work of Man Ray. He was cameraman, director, editor and the sound accompaniment was his choice of phonograph records of the day. Nothing less than complete authorship of a work interests him. Collaboration would dilute his freedom as artist. In speaking of his insistence upon sole authorship of his works, he told me, without cracking a trace of a smile, "I never collaborate with more than one person at a time, and then only for pleasure." I also learned that the films were shot without preliminary scripts, evolving as he went along in order to take full advantage of chance and of improvisation. Ironically, when he was in Hollywood during the Forties, the magnates of the motion picture industry failed to employ his remarkable gifts as a film maker. Short of funds at the time, if given the chance and a free hand, he almost certainly would have added luster to the history of film in America.

Man Ray the person is just as elusive, just as much a paradox, as Man Ray the artist. Even though the full story of his life can be found in his autobiography, *Self Portrait*, published in 1963, certain aspects of his personality are worth noting here. A Parisian since 1921, Man Ray remains American to the core. Encountering him in Paris, one senses instantly that his American roots are as firm and vigorous as they were forty odd years ago. Paradoxically, when he was in

The Rope Dancer Accompanies Herself with Her Shadows, 1916
Oil
$52 \times 73^3/_8''$
Collection The Museum of Modern Art, Gift of G. David Thompson
(not in exhibition)

Hollywood during the Second World War and for a few years thereafter, he was as much an expatriate on these shores as his friends Max Ernst and André Breton. Like them, he was forced to take refuge in America at that disruptive juncture in history. There are other enigmas. One — the spirited playfulness in his legendary wit and in much of his work as an artist, yet, on acquaintance, he usually is grave, reserved, saturnine, almost dour. Another — the fraternization, in his work, thought and conversation, of poetic flights of imagination with analytical intelligence. It is as if René Descartes and Hieronymous Bosch were one and the same. Finally — in keeping with his Dada approach to life, he scorns and derides modern civilization, yet he is one of the most civilized men of our time.

The most illuminating clue to Man Ray the artist and Man Ray the person — mirror images of one another — can be found in his Dada attitude to art and life. It has been fifty years since the Dada attitude to art and life first was articulated by a handful of expatriate poets and artists from several corners of Europe at the Cab-

Portrait of the artist with shaving cream
Paris
1953
Photograph by Mrs. Man Ray

aret Voltaire in Zurich during the darkest days of the First World War. At that moment, the superstructure of Western Civilization appeared to have collapsed. Sanguine faith in the rule of reason had been undermined by the horrors of technological warfare. The notion that mankind was destined to progress ever onward and upward was seen by the poets and artists at the Cabaret Voltaire as a fraudulent snare and delusion.

The youthful Dadaists who took over the Cabaret Voltaire — among them Hugo Ball, Tristan Tzara, Hans Arp and Marcel Janco — believed it was time for a wholly new beginning in their efforts as artists and in their view of life in the modern world. They were convinced that existing systems of thought had failed in large measure because thought in science and philosophy was systematized. In the arts, they opposed the regulation of creative endeavor by codified rules of any kind. In place of the Rule of Reason, they favored the Whims of Chance. Moreover, they asserted that the artist contaminates the sensibility unique to himself to the extent he adheres to doctrines, credos, conventions, authority.

From that slant, the institutional structure of art was seen as obsolete. Museums, academies, art schools, contending movements, the sanctifications of art history, the pecking order infesting the art world were considered to be vestigial absurdities. It is in this sense that Dada was anti-art. The Dadaists jeered Culture with a capital C, Art with a capital A. They believed that by removing art from the hurly-burly of life and installing it as something sacred, the vital experience of art was transformed into a mandate of what one ought to feel and enjoy. Anti-art in this sense is not the same as the rejection of art per se. After all, the Dadaists went on making works of art, writing poems, staging performances at the Cabaret Voltaire that today would be described as music hall Happenings. They refused, however, to conform to any stylistic procedure, including any approach they themselves might enunciate. That being the case, there is no such thing as an identifiable Dada style.

The procedures of dividing art into schools, movements, epochs, countries, regions and stylistic tendencies of one sort or another are the stock in trade of critics and art historians. Dada rejected these procedures. Consequently, the Dadaists repudiated the endorsement of critics and art historians. Each work of art, they affirmed, must be contemplated as an entity unto itself. Its connections with other works are incidental, not essential. The Dada artist could, accordingly, con-

16

ceive his work in any way he wished, including the fashioning of images in some accredited style, if that suited his fancy, or to cross boundaries between styles thought to be distinctive from each other. In short, no holds were barred. Such are the perverse effects of time, Dada now is a respectable designation employed by art critics, and it enjoys an esteemed place in the studies of art historians.

Dada freedom with reference to style appears again and again in the works of Man Ray. One cannot stylistically identify a work as indisputably by him. Nor would he be gratified if one could. He refuses to play the game according to the rules proclaimed by critics and art historians. Even in his Surrealist days, from the middle of the Twenties to the onset of the Second World War, he avoided conformity to doctrines of the movement. He retained a Dada independence throughout the Surealist period, creating works from time to time that do not accord with the principles of that school. For Man Ray, the making of works of art, is not work in the burdensome sense. He has said, "Everything I do is done in the spirit of pleasure. Sometimes my work is physically hard work. Mentally, it's pure pleasure." The equation of work and pleasure is a Dada attitude and it has characterized Man Ray for a half-century or longer.

Another side of Dada provides clues to Man Ray — its delight in the enigma, in the inexplicable, in mystification. On more than one occasion he has remarked to the writer that a work of art which can be taken apart and put together as if it was some kind of machine holds no interest for him. What does engage his interest in a work of art are those facets which defy analysis and are imbued with mystery. This applies to his own efforts as well as to the creations of others. In the preface to a proposed book, titled *One Hundred Objects of My Affection*, he says,

"In assembling *Objects of My Affection,* the author indulged in an activity parallel to his painting and photography, an activity which he hopes will elude criticism and evaluation. These objects are a mystery to himself as much as they might be to others, and he hopes they will always remain so. That is their justification, if any is needed.

We all love a mystery, but must it necessarily be murder?"

This kind of mystification applies to Man Ray the person. There is about him something of the conjurer, the prestidigitator enveloped by the strange, the anomalous, the unexpected.

One more aspect of Dada appealing to Man Ray was its glee in the spoof, its spirited hi-jinks, its refusal to be pompous. It is no wonder he found his milieu in Paris in 1921 when he was welcomed with open arms by Tristan Tzara, Max Ernst, Marcel Duchamp and the other Dadaists who had preceded him there. On the occasion of his first Paris exhibition, shortly after his arrival, they presented him to the public as an enigma. The catalog they prepared for his show at Libraire Six was headed *Good News*. It stated, among other things, that it was not known where the artist was born, and that after a career as a coal merchant, several times millionaire, and chairman of the chewing gum trust, he accepted the invitation of the Dadaists to show his recent paintings. It is the kind of introduction Man Ray could have engineered himself.

When Man Ray arrived in Paris he was the acknowledged American prototype of Dada. By 1921 Dada had sprung from Zurich to Cologne, Berlin, Paris and New York. Indeed, about the same time in 1916 when the young poets and artists in Zurich were taking over the Cabaret Voltaire, Marcel Duchamp and Man Ray in New York were taking similar positions with regard to art and life, unaware there was a Zurich group calling itself Dada. They became aware of the Zurich development upon the arrival in New York of the painter Francis Picabia from war-torn Europe. Marcel Duchamp and Man Ray contributed in New York to Picabia's publication, *391*, and subsequently the two edited the sole issue of *New York Dada*. Shortly afterward, Marcel Duchamp, and then Man Ray, departed for Paris.

Through the years, Man Ray has known and been a close friend of many distinguished persons in the arts. Of all these, his most enduring and meaningful friendship hab been with Duchamp. They have influenced each other in numerous and subtle ways, and for half-a-century they have retained, without diminuition, their high regard for one another. When they meet, on occasions when Duchamp is in Paris, or Man Ray in New York, or during the Summer at Cadaques on the Costa Brava in Spain, they play chess and resume the conversation of their last encounter. It is a unique and consequential friendship in the annals of modern art.

As for Man Ray's participation in Surrealism, he was inspirited by such ideas of that movement as the significance of the dream, the unconscious, chance, accident, free association, and by the attraction of the surrealists to the mysterious and the disquieting. Such surrealist works by him as the series entitled *Shakespearean Equations* are suffused with the inexplicable. At the same time, he introduced into the *Shakespearean Equations* an ironic Dada element in the juxtaposition of rational mathematical structures (he had seen in three-dimensional form at the Poincaré Institute in Paris) and irrational images sprung from the depths of his unconscious. His closest attachment among the surrealists in Paris was with the poet Paul Éluard. They issued two volumes of verse and illustrations — *Facile* in 1935, with photographs by Man Ray, and *Les Mains libres* in 1937, with drawings by the artist. While the surrealist years account for many of the artist's finest works, those accomplishments are in many ways an extension of his Dada attitudes to art and life.

It is forty-five years since Man Ray, the young Dadaist, came to Paris for the first time. In matters that count, he is as Dada now as then. He persists in being purely and simply himself, going on with his work for the pure pleasure it gives him. It is in that spirit that this exhibition has been organized — for the pure pleasure viewers may derive from direct encounter with his works.

Self Portrait, 1936
Ink
$11 \times 8^3/_4''$
Collection Mr. and Mrs. David Savage, Princeton, New Jersey

man Ray 1936 n.y.

Man Ray on Man Ray

An Autobiography

When I arrived in France for the first time in 1921, the Dadaists declared that no one knew where I was born. They also did not know that I almost was not born at all. My parents separated one week after they were married, and met again by chance one week later. Only then did they agree to bring me into this world. It has definitely been established that I was born in Philadelphia in 1890.

It seems that I began to paint at the age of seven, to everyone's consternation. I escaped to New York and after having run through several fortunes as a coal merchant, chairman of the chewing gum trust, modern architect and banjo player, I returned to my first love, painting, and have been faithful ever since. Unfortunately (for the others) I have never until recently and too late received official recognition, but Max Ernst's prophecy that I would always find buyers has come true. He said I have always attached the cursed handle to a broom sporting a hammer.

Any deviations I have been guilty of can in no way distract a doting public, since they are extremely personal and cannot be discussed with decorum in this outline.

From the catalog of the exhibition,
Pasadena Art Institute, 1944

What I Am

Everyone will tell you that I am not a painter. That is true. Since the beginning of my career, I was at once classed among the photometrographers. My works are pure photometrography. Take *Revolving Doors* or *Seguidilla*, *Le Beau Temps* or *The Shakespearian Equations*, you will notice that no plastic idea entered into the creation of these works. It is scientific thought which dominates. Besides, I take greater pleasure in measuring a color than in looking at it. Holding a photometer, I work joyfully and surely. What is there that I have not weighed or measured? All Uccello, all Leonardo, etc. It's very strange. The first time I used a photoscope I examined a pear of medium size. I assure you I never saw anything more repulsive. I called my servant and showed it to her. On the photo-scale an ordinary common nude weighed 200 pounds. It had been produced by a very fat painter whom I also weighed. Are you familiar with the cleaning of colors? It is quite filthy. Spinning is cleaner. Knowing how to classify them is very delicate and needs good sight. Here we are face to face with phototechnicology. As for abstract explosions, so often annoying, cotton wool placed on the eyes will attenuate them suitably. Here we arrive at pyrophotology. To draw my *Mains Libres* I used a caleido-photorecorder. This took seven minutes. I called my servant and showed it to her. I think I may say that photology is superior to painting. It is more varied. The pecunary yield is greater. I owe to it my fortune. Anyhow, with a monodymanophot a barely trained photo-measurer can record in the same time with the same effort more colors than the most adept painter. It is thanks to this that I have painted so much. The future belongs to philophotology.   (With the help of Erik Satie)
From the catalog of the exhibition,
Institute of Contemporary Art, London, 1959

The Age of Light

In this Age, like all ages, when the problem of a perpetuation of a race or class and the destruction of its enemies, is the all-absorbing motive of civilized society, it seems irrelevant and wasteful still to create works whose only inspirations are individual human emotion and desire. The attitude seems to be that one may be permitted a return to the idyllic occupations

Merry Wives of Windsor, 1948
Oil   24 × 18″
Cordier & Ekstrom, Inc., New York

only after meriting this return by solving the more vital problems of existence. Still, we know that the incapacity of race or class to improve itself is as great as its incapacity to learn from previous errors in history. All progress results from an intense individual desire to improve the immediate present, from an all-conscious sense of material insufficiency. In this exalted state, material action imposes itself and takes the form of revolution in one form or another. Race and class, like styles, then become irrelevant, while the emotion of the human individual becomes universal. For what can be more binding amongst beings than than the discovery of a common desire? And what can be more inspiring to action than the confidence aroused by a lyric expression of this desire? From the first gesture of a child pointing to an object and simply naming it, but with a world of intended meaning, to the developed mind that creates an image whose strangeness and reality stirs our subconscious to its inmost depths, the awakening of desire is the first step to participation and experience.

It is in the spirit of an experience and not of experiment that the following autobiographical images are presented. Seized in moments of visual detachment during periods of emotional contact, these images are oxidized residues, fixed by light and chemical elements, of living organisms. No plastic expression can ever be more than a residue of an experience. The recognition of an image that has tragically survived an experience, recalling the event more or less clearly, like the undisturbed ashes of an object consumed by flames, the recognition of this object so little representative and so fragile, and its simple identification on the part of the spectator with a similar personal experience, precludes all psycho-analytical classification or assimilation into an arbitrary decorative system. Questions of merit and of execution can always be taken care of by those who hold themselves aloof from even the frontiers of such experiences. For, whether a painter, emphasizing the importance of the idea he wishes to convey introduces bits of ready-made chromos alongside his handiwork, or whether another, working directly with light and chemistry, so deforms the subject as almost to hide the identity of the original, and creates a new form, the ensuing violation of the medium employed is the most perfect assurance of the author's convictions. A certain amount of contempt for the material employed to express an idea is indispensable to the purest realization of this idea.

Each one of use, in his timidity, has a limit beyond which he is outraged. It is inevitable that he who by concentrated application has extended this limit to himself, should arouse the resentment of those who, since accepted by all, require no initiative of application. And this resentment generally takes the form of meaningless laughter or of criticism, if not of persecution. But this apparent violation is preferable to the monstrous habits condoned by etiquette and estheticism.

An effort impelled by desire must also have an automatic or subconscious energy to aid its realization. The reserves of this energy within us are limitless if we will draw on them without a sense of shame or of propriety. Like the scientist who is merely a prestidigitator manipulating the abundant phenomena of nature and profiting by every so called hazard or law, by his own selectivity, which is universal desire, and exposes to the light motives and instincts long repressed, which should form the basis of a confident fraternity. The intensity of this message can be disturbing only in proportion to the freedom that has been given to automatism or the subconscious self. The removal of inculcated modes of presentation, resulting in apparent artificialty or strangeness, is a confirmation of the free functioning of this automatism and is to be welcomed.

Open confidences are being made every day, and it remains for the eye to train itself to see them without prejudice or restraint.   1934

From *Photographies, 1920–1934, Paris*

A Note on the Shakespearean Equations

About twelve years ago when Max Ernst first called my attention to the mathematical objects languishing in the dusty cases of the Poincaré Institute in Paris, I took new courage in my resolve to seek inspiration as much as possible from man-made objects. It is true that at the time many expressed doubts as to their utilization for their creative value. "It would be," said André Breton, "falling into the trap of closed rationalism to oppose mathematical objects with their arid formulas to poetical objects with more seductive titles. Let us observe, in passing, that the thought which gave them life stemmed from the surest of procedures, from the abstract toward the concrete, whereas a branch of contemporary art (Abstraction) persists in the opposite direction, and risks, by the publication of such documents (mathematical objects), to see its realizations definitely outclassed. Now that these almost unknown objects have been brought to our attention, it remains for us to interpret them in our own manner, in order to appropriate them. For my part, I propose to substitute for the original analytical titles these intentionally more elementary ones, but humanly more evocative: *Pursued by her Hoop, Death of the Paper Favor, Thus Spake . . ., The Floe, Russian Campaign, The Round Knife, Hypnotic Sleep, The Tournament, the Rose Penitents, Ring of the Rose Bush, The Circus, The Abandoned Novel, etc.*" It had been my intention to ask Breton, since he had been among the first to consider this subject, to provide me with an introduction in the form of a letter, for my final realization of the mathematical equations. On second thought I feel that I should use *my* letter to *him* as a foreword. Here it is:

My dear André,

Let me reassure you, I have always been in accord with you on the necessity of perverting the legitimate legends of the mathematical objects, if we are to consider these as a valid source of inspiration. I also wish to assure you that the objects were never intended to serve as a projection of or a justification for abstract art. I did take a certain diabolical pleasure in the discomfiture and impotence they worked on the exponents of non-objective art with whom my principal quarrel is the poverty of inventiveness and imagination. It is of significance to me that in last year's Surrealist show in Paris, and in the separate abstract show some of the same exhibitors participated. Some of the most respected ones, I mean, like Arp and Picabia. I should have done likewise if I had had the opportunity. You know me; I exhibit upon any unconditional invitation, anywhere; I like to carry my propaganda into the enemy's camp. It is the only effective propaganda. We do not need to convert those who are already on our side.

"Oh austere mathematics! I have not forgotten you . . ." sings Lautréamont in his second canto wherein there is very little of mathematics and one of the most powerful indictments of man's follies and obsessions ever recorded: "Your modest pyramids will endure longer than the pyramids of Egypt, those ant-hills erected by stupidity and slavery." It has always been a model for me, this passage, of the employment of an irrelevant subject for the declaration of a conviction and for a denunciation. And so it has been for me, with every line drawn, with every area of color applied; as if I were soaring over the land dropping bright-colored leaflets containing songs to not only distract but to set a pattern for a more generous world. A large order, you say, my friend, but isn't that what you, too, have been doing all these years?

In returning to the mathematical objects as a source of material for my "Shakespearean Equations," I proposed to myself not only to take liberties with the legends, but with the forms themselves, their composition, and by the addition of color, to make them as arbitrary as the most creative work could be. I was as free to do this any painter of fruit or faces is free to choose his subject.

I do hope that my choice of the titles is as free and automatic as is yours, quoted earlier; I could have used yours if I had had enough to cover the series. There is not a great difference, however, between your "Thus spake..." and my "Othello." And when one looks at the painting, the difference is even less noticeable.

Whatever our divergences have been, I feel our make-up and our continuity (as we say here in Hollywood) has been unaffected; I draw this conclusion from the dedication to me in your last book: I am, you say, "the same as I found you in 1920, the rest is misery."

Always yours sincerely,
Man Ray

From the portfolio of the exhibition, *To Be Continued Unnoticed*, Copley Galleries, Beverly Hills, 1948

Man Ray on Man Ray

To be Continued Unnoticed

Of all the questions asked, "how do you do it?" is the one that should provoke the least response on the part of an artist. Now, if you ask me simply, "*what* are you doing," I am all smiles and accommodating. I proceed at once to unload all my treasures and secret desires even to the point of satiety, little caring whether in the end I shall exhaust you as well as my own patience. Rather have the questioner go away surfeited and wobbly, than to have him stare between two works and ask again, "is that all, no more?" One is not sure whether he has not had enough or whether he is merely being polite. So I take no chances.

Pleasure, and the pursuit of freedom are the guiding motives in all human activity. The pursuit of freedom is work; the pursuit of pleasure is the play, all learned opinions to the contrary. All criticism is destructive, most of all self-criticism. All work and all play are the signature of their authors. Would you have me change my signature, or my sex? But the world is full, is reeking with elements to suit *your* tastes and *your* desires. There is room for all.

That most subversive of human activity, competition, exists the least in creative work. The artist is the only

Mirror to Die Laughing By, 1952
Mixed media object
Collection Mr. and Mrs. Morton G. Neumann, Chicago

true sage. He comes to us with open mind and with open hands. When his work confronts others he is not up for trial, it is the spectator, if anyone, who is putting himself on record. Time has proven this again and again.

They tell us that what distinguishes the human race from other species, what makes it superior, is its capacity of laughter. But I have seen donkeys and monkeys laughing themselves into hysteria. Watching the human race. No, what distinguishes our race, and only through a few representatives of it, is a capacity for creating gratuitous emblems. As if we were gods freed from the necessity of survival. Science might be included in this activity.

But art is not science. Art is not an experiment. There is no progress in art, any more than there is progress in making love. There are simply different ways of doing it. There may be a certain progress in the individual, but his signature remains unchanged.

When the spirit moves me, I use a stick with some hairs on it. I become a painter. My barber and the violinist above me also use sticks with hairs on them. We have much in common. We are also different. They try to do their work as well as possible. I simply try to be as free as possible. In my manner of working; in the choice of my subject. No one can dictate to me or guide me. They may criticize me afterwards, but it is too late. The work is done. I have tasted freedom. It was also hard work, but it was worth it.

Never have I submitted my work knowingly or willingly to a jury, not even to one whose members I might judge qualified to pass upon it. Take it or leave it, I say. Say anything you like behind my back. If you say it to my face, I may spit in yours. How would I handle the hordes who wish to exhibit themselves? Very simply: by lottery, or for a fee. The first is fairer. I don't think it has been tried. Ah yes, but there are prizes to award. That, too, is simple — by lottery. But, you say, if the one who perpetrates the worst work wins the first prize, where are we? Gentlemen, have you no charity, no generosity? The culprit deserves compensation for his miserable effort, he deserves consolation. And, if by chance the one you might have awarded the prize to, anyway, wins it, what a triumph for your judgment! See how many have been condemned by your approval, as it is. However, we have other consolations, for instance: all opinion is transient, and all work is permanent.

Man Ray

From the portfolio of the exhibition, *To Be Continued Unnoticed*, Copley Galleries, Beverly Hills, 1948

DADAMADE

Who made Dada? Nobody and everybody. I made Dada when I was a baby and I was roundly spanked by my mother. Now, everyone claims to be the author of Dada. For the past thirty years. In Zurich, in Cologne, in Paris, in London, in Tokyo, in San Francisco, in New York I might claim to be the author of Dada in New York. In 1912 before Dada. In 1919, with the permission and with the approval of other Dadaists I legalized Dada in New York. Just once! That was enough. The times did not deserve more. That was a Dadadate. The one issue of New York Dada did not even bear the names of its authors. How unusual for Dada! Of course, there were a certain number of collaborators. Both willing and unwilling. Both trusting and suspicious! What did it matter? Only one issue. Forgotten — not even seen by most Dadaists or antidadaists. Now, we are trying to revive Dada.

From the catalog of the exhibition, *Dada*, Kunstverein
für die Rheinlande und Westfalen, Düsseldorf, 1958

Why? Who cares? Who doesn't care?
Dada is dead. Or is Dada still alive?
We cannot revive something that is
alive just as we cannot revive any-
thing that is dead.
Is Dadadead?
Is Dadalive?
Dada is.
Dadaism

Man Ray
Ramatuelle, Var, France
July 8, 1958

The Rayograph 1920—1928

Forty years ago when forty copies of *Les Champs dé-licieux* appeared with the first rayographs, a positive step was taken to put a curb on the prolific productions in all art mediums.

"But let us speak of art," said Tristan at the time, "yes, art. I know a gentleman who makes excellent portraits. This gentleman is a camera. But, says you, color is lacking as well as the trembling of the brush. This uncertain shiver at first was a weakness which, to justify itself called itself sensitiveness. It seems that human imperfection has more serious qualities than the precision of machines. And what about still-lifes? I should like to know if hors-d'œuvres, desserts and the baskets of game do not better attract the breath of our appetite ... Why does not one make a portrait of all this? ... When all that which is called art was well covered with rheumatism, the photographer turned on the thousand candle-power of his lamp and by degrees the sensitive paper absorbed the black silhouetted by ordinary objects. He had invented the force of a tender and fresh flash which exceeded in importance all the constellations destined for our visual pleasures. The mechanical deformation, precise, unique, and right was fixed, smooth and filtered like hair through a comb of light."

In other words, by another poet: "There are as many marvels in a glass of wine as at the bottom of the sea."

There is, however, this consideration which obsesses the artist: how to reduce the clutter of objects and works of art that fill the world, like populations which increase despite the endless destruction as practised by nature (of which man is a part).

One of the solutions is to reduce all art forms to a two-dimensional monochrome like this page of words. More and more every day from a simple preface to

heavy volumes, visual works are accompanied by words that try to justify these works.

"But," says you as always, "color is lacking." What can compare to a peach or a cloud gradually blushing under the rays of the sun during a prolonged exposure? A dimension, the time element, never attained by the static arts. They seize only the result.

Like the undisturbed ashes of an object consumed by flames these images are oxidized residues fixed by light and chemical elements of an experience, an adventure, not an experiment. They are the result of curiosity, inspiration, and these words do not pretend to convey any information.

Paris, February 1963

From the portfolio of the exhibition,
Rayographs 1921—1928, LGA-Ausstellung,
Stuttgart, 1963

Rayograph
date unknown
Collection Mr. and Mrs. Man Ray, Paris

Rayograph
date unknown
Collection Mr. and Mrs. Man Ray, Paris

27

I Have Never Painted a Recent Picture

Little did I foresee when I made useless objects with useful titles like *Boardwalk, Lampshade* or *Object To Be Destroyed* that others would take the titles literally. *Boardwalk* was laid on the ground and walked upon, an electric bulb was inserted in the *Lampshade* and the metronome with ticking eye. *To Be Destroyed,* was destroyed by literal minded spirits.

Fortunately, upon demand, it was simple enough to reconstruct these objects despite the disapproval of those who valued only originals. Is a book or a bronze an original? I leave such considerations to well intentioned collectors and amateurs of the rare. These can always concentrate on painting whose duplication is more difficult and more easily discernible.

Speaking of painting, let me tell you a little secret. In view of the increasing demand for such originals I have constructed a machine involving fifty pantographs that will duplicate a painting in the process of creation as easily as a president can sign fifty checks with one flourish. This however, might create a new species of collectors who would compare notes (paintings, not checks) in order to discern slight differences which would distinguish one work from another, thus making them all originals.

Now, let us speak seriously (meaningless word concealing so many subterfuges) of painting and its derivatives. Or rather, let us not speak of painting — leave it to those who do not paint. Painters should be seen, not heard, they say. But this does not prevent the painter from feeling and thinking in terms of communicable words indispensable, it seems, to all the more esoteric forms of creation. However, the spectator can nowadays dispense with words. Dates, names or the recency of the work are adequate commentaries for him.

When asked to show his latest work — as if he were a fashion designer creating a new style for the season, to be set aside the following year for the newer style, also to be forgotten — when asked to show his latest work, the painter is overcome by a feeling of futility as if all his previous work has been discarded. He knows that much

Imaginary Portrait of D. A. F. de Sade, 1938
Oil
$21^5/_8 \times 17^3/_4''$
Private Collection

afin que... les traces de ma tombe disparaissent de dessus de la surface de la terre, comme je me flatte que ma mémoire s'effacera de l'esprit des hommes... D.A.F. SADE.

DANCE

MAN RAY
1915

later the dates will be meaningless and only the signature will count—if he is still "rated." In any case posterity is not his concern. History and statistics are meaningless to him.

Then there is the question of influences. All creators are influenced if they are aware by what has been done before. Otherwise they would be naïve or primitive like the Sunday painters who have never entered a museum nor opened a book. The outer limits of time and space are beyond our reach today. We can only gain inspiration from the few thousand years of our knowledge of the creations of the human race, to create equally valid works in the spirit of our time which later may appear as primitive as the works in the museums and caves. But this, too, is not the creator's concern.

We are a race or rather a species whose peculiarity is to accumulate. In contrast with all the other species in nature. We seek variety in life—in art, in food, etcetera. Are we therefore superior? A meaningless word, like the word serious—I doubt all evaluations.

The pursuit of pleasure, of liberty and the realization of individuality are also unique motives of the human race, only possible of attainment in our present society through creative work.

Man Ray

Written for this catalog   Paris 1966

Dance, 1915
Oil
36 x 28″
Private Collection

Man Ray

L'orage d'une robe qui s'abat
Puis un corps simple sans nuages
Ainsi venez me dire tous vos charmes
Vous qui avez eu votre part de bonheur
Et qui pleurez souvent le sort sinistre de celui
    qui vous a rendue si heureuse
Vous qui n'avez pas envie de raisonner
Vous qui n'avez pas su faire un homme
Sans en aimer un autre

Dans les espaces de marées d'un corps qui se dévêt
A la mamelle du crépuscule ressemblant
L'œil fait la chaîne sur les dunes négligées
Où les fontaines tiennent dans leurs griffes
    des mains nues
Vestiges du front nu joues pâles sous les cils de l'horizon
Une larme fusée fiancée au passé
Savoir que la lumière fut fertile
Des hirondelles enfantines prennent la terre pour le ciel

La chambre noire où tous les cailloux du froid sont à vif
Ne dis pas que tu n'as pas peur
Ton regard est à hauteur de mon épaule
Tu es trop belle pour prêcher la chasteté

Dans la chambre noire où le blé même
Naît de la gourmandise

Reste immobile
Et tu es seule

                Paul Éluard

Man Ray

The storm of a robe which falls
Then a simple body without clouds
So come and tell me all your charms
You who have had your share of happiness
And who often bewails the dismal fate of the one
    who made you so happy
You who have no desire to reason
You who knew not how to create a man
Without loving another

In the ebb and flow of a body which undresses
Akin to the breast of twilight
The eye forms in line on the neglected dunes
Where the fountains hold naked hands within their claws
Vestiges of bare forehead pale cheeks beneath the
    eyelashes of the horizon
A rocket-like tear betrothed to the past
To know that light was fertile
Childish swallows mistake the earth for the sky

The dark room where the stones of cold are bare
Do not say you have no fear
Your look is level with my shoulder
You are too lovely to preach chastity

In the dark room where even the wheat
Is born of greedinees

Remain unmoving
And you are alone

                Paul Éluard

Man Ray's Friends on Man Ray

La vie en ose

on suppose
on oppose
on impose
on dépose
on repose
on indispose

    et Finalement une dose de Ménopause
     AVEC osmose
      sclérose
     et ankylose
       MAIS la chose qui ose
    pour Man Ray
      Marcel Duchamp 1963

From the announcement of the exhibition, Cordier & Ekstrom, Inc., New York, 1963

Man Ray

Le trappeur en chambre
Le duveteur des raisins de la vue
Le capteur de soleil et l'exalteur d'ombres
Le grand scrutateur du décor de la vie quotidienne
Le boussolier du jamais vu le naufrageur du prévu
Le prince du déclic
Le matinier du goût
Le plafonneur des élégances
Le pilote de ses cerfs-volants — lèvres et cœurs —
 au-dessus de nos toits
Le dévideur de l'air en autant de serpentins de
 Riemann
Le désespoir du perroquet
Le joueur impassible
Mon ami Man Ray
    André Breton
    Source and date unknown

Man Ray

The trapper indoors
The furrier of the grapes of sight
The catcher of the sun and celebrant of shadows
The grand inquisitor of life's trappings
The pilot of the never seen, shipwrecker of the
 predictable
The prince of the shutter
The herald of taste
The flyer of kites-lips and hearts-above our roofs
The separator of air in the serpentines of Riemann
The despair of the parrot
The impassive gambler
My friend Man Ray
    André Breton

Translation by Anna Bruni Seldis

Men Before the Mirror

Rrose Sélavy 1934

Many a time the mirror imprisons them and holds them firmly. Fascinated they stand in front. They are absorbed, separated from reality and alone with their dearest vice, vanity. However readily they spread out all other vices for all, they keep this one secret and disown it even before their most intimate friends.

There they stand and stare at the landscape which is themselves, the mountains of their noses, the defiles and folds of their shoulders, hands and skin, to which the years have already so accustomed them that they no longer know how they evolved; and the multiple primeval forests of their hair. They meditate, they are content, they try to take themselves in as a whole. Certain traits appear too small, and it is well so, but others are too large and it is magnificent so. Women have taught them that power does not succeed. Women have told them what is attractive in them, they have forgotten; but now they put themselves together like a mosaic out of what pleased women in them. For they themselves do not know what is attractive about them. Only handsome men are sure of themselves, but handsome men are not fitted for love: they wonder even at the last moment whether it suits them. Fitted for love are the great ugly things that carry their faces with pride before them like a mask. The great taciturns, who behind their silence hide much or nothing.

Slim hands with long fingers or short, that grasp forth. The nape of a neck that rises steeply to lose itself in the forest's edge of the hair, the tender curve of the skin behind an ear, the mysterious mussel of the navel, the flat pebbles of the knee caps, the joints of their ankles, which a hand envelops to hold them back from a leap — and beyond the farther and still unknown region of the body, much older than it, much more worn, open to all happenings: this face, always this face which they know so well. For they have a body only at night and most only in the arms of a woman. But with them goes always, ever present their face.

The mirror looks at them. They collect themselves. Carefully, as if tying a cravat, they compose their features. Insolent, serious and conscious of their looks they turn around to face the world.

From *Photographies, 1920—1934, Paris*

THE visages of THE woman

André Breton 1934

Bright faces brought together out of time, faces of living women. I am seated on a bench in the springtime to see pass in a dream this tramway color of vapor rising from the fields, an admirable head in each window. All that, which is most perfect hour the most perfect street in the world cannot give, is called upon to precipitate here, beyond every obstacle, its luminous career. The most perfect street in the world? Rather that of today than ever. The nocturnal signs have not in vain confused their letters of fire in the tresses of dark violets or of pearls. The draft of very low cars has not, once for all, bitten on the lengths of these tresses, but what a little below the ear behold them free to curl, ready to flutter at the slightest movement. Nor is the ear which they in turn cover and uncover, any longer exactly the same since it expects to be sought after from elsewhere, from no matter what other part of the world, instantly capable of destroying that part. I shall not try to set forth what these eyes have seen, which was invisible for others, whereby I am most generally subjugated in them. No matter, it is clear that their burning is stronger than that of all eyes of the past, stronger not only because they unconsciously reflect a human existence which, for us, is and will remain its last stage, — the sciences, the arts, all means of seduction, fashion, philosophies, the present tendency of morals — but above all because our own eyes burning concretely with the same flame, are subject to be enchanted, dazzled, filled with tears before these eyes. These quivering nostrils, these trembling lips, these swelling throats — it is a whole communion of perfumes, of thoughts and of breathing which attach us to these beings as to no others making us feel again the best we have known: the awakening of our heart in the very heart of this century. These attitudes, wonderfully instinctive, are the first they knew how to take; each of them is a total of desires and dreams which have never before been had and which never will again. In the repose and silence of a few seconds, light and shade have served to model these perfect incarnations not only of what is most modern in poetry, music and the dance as of what is most eternally young in the art of love.

It is of Man Ray alone that we may expect the real *Ballad of Women of the present Day* of which it is possible to give only an extract in this collection. Indeed, it is not a pledge to wish to surprise human beauty in movement at the very point where it reaches its full power: so sure of itself as to appear to ignore itself! It needed the eye of a great hunter, the patience, the sense of the moment pathetically right when a balance, transient besides, occured in the expression of a face, between dream and action. It needed nothing less than the admirable experience which, in the vastest plastic domain, is that of Man Ray, to dare beyond the immediate likeness — which is often only that of a day or of certain days — to aim for the profound likeness which physically, morally engages the entire future. The portrait of a loved one should not be only an image at which one smiles but aslo an oracle one questions. In short, it needed all the sparkling curiosity, all the indomitable audacity which, besides, characterizes the intellectual effort of Man Ray, in order that, out of so many contradictory and charming features which he chooses to give us, the one being composes itself in whom we are given to see the last incarnation of the Sphinx.

From *Photographies, 1920—1934, Paris*

When Things Dream

Tristan Tzara 1934

Along this promenade which joins the ends of days to the ends of nights, indefatigably present, whose length cannot be measured in spite of a suspicion of limits barely offered to our minds, along this promenade where the ends of days joined to the ends of nights succeed to detach themselves to drag miserably adrift of tunnels, from wreck to wreck, castaways of blindness, we perceive the period of life, the period of joys and greatnesses, of despair and of slaveries, within reach of our fixed looks, within reach of compact and fine masses, infinitely sweet to the doubt that follows us along, we perceive objects. By dint of going from sea to mountain the caress is finally torn apart like the wave, henceforth dwells therein the secret of certitude. Imperceptibly profound are the perspectives of this rent, for it calls forth sorrow, its constant companion, and it is only around it, in the flowing circles caused by a stone in clear weather of water and moon, — or by the eddies of a train launched at full speed in the sky, — that life no longer seeks its wherefore and resigns itself to its combustion without shadow nor after-taste. It is not so much the reality of matter and its problematic solidity, as its representation of landmarks to designate space, making us conscious of it through time and our own existence, which attaches the thing of representative form to our mental life. Submarine views, stones of clouds, flights of sharks by waves of applause, retinas of veils, auroras of crustaceans in glass, tables of direction, watches of lightening, crumpled papers that trouble the stars and the thousand feathers of resentment, all that which awakens tenderness out of all reason, unstable flames, sisters of love (the very indifference we often show towards them is the guarantee of a great peace, certitude), from childhood until death do you people this ocean which you accompany with your supreme silence, the feeling which selects you according to the indestructible appearances and the infinitely varying forms of the laws of nature. Things to touch, to eat, to crunch, to apply to the eye, to the skin, to press, to lick, to break, to grind, things to lie, to flee from, to honor, things cold or hot, feminine or masculine, things of day or night which absorb through your pores the greater part of our life, that which expresses itself unnoticed, that which matters because it does not know itself and spends itself without reckoning on the thousand load-stones placed along the edge of the unanimous road, your slumbers fixed in a case of butterflies have cut the diamond under all the aspects of the earth, in out childhoods lost inside of ourselves and unspeakably loaded with dreams like the geological layers that serve us as bed sheets.

Flight opened in a cut of flesh above the unused delight of conflagrations of midnight: it is experience consuming itself with its unavowed impotence. Thirst reabsorbs itself ever cloudy and the contours of the routes of flesh stem from an ever limpid vigilance and form the hills where the vegetations group themselves into marine clots in the form of sponges and microscopic navigations of blood and alcohol.

Thus, in the fixed course of the universe which inscribes itself with cruelty into the psychic life of each one of us, establishes itself the contradiction of man, which sees in each step on the moving stairway, a familiar utensil, loved or indifferent, whereas the continuity of life does not encumber itself with the materialism of facts, for it is merely waves and imperceptible transitions of rounded angles. And this continuity possesses its own world which fills the land of beaming shadows with the most beautiful memories of caresses, of the dead and of emotions — so that one can never keep silent enough on the face of this earth. These are projections surprised in transparence, by the light of tenderness, of things that dream and talk in their sleep.   From *Photographies, 1920—1934, Paris*

Mr. Knife and Miss Fork,
1944
Mixed media object
$13^{1}/_{2} \times 9^{3}/_{4}$″
Collection Mr. and
Mrs. David Savage,
Princetown, New Jersey

37

Where Pencils Are Made, 1936
Ink
Collection Mr. and Mrs. Man Ray, Paris

Notes on the Drawings of Man Ray

Paul Éluard 1936

Look well at these drawings and tell me if these sensitive traits, if these endless lines do not seem to be traced by the trembling of an untiring heart, by the particular drifting of overpowering ideas surging out of very precious desires.

Behind each invention, each discovery, search out desire, not necessity.

These leaves of paper were white nights. Under the hand of Man Ray, they blush, like innocents. They reflect anxiety and ardor.

Here beings live on the edge of light, on the shores so often empty, of the dreaming eye.

In these drawings a world is offered to us, a man reveals himself, he gives us his eyes, his hands. There are as many marvels in a glass of wine at at the bottom of the sea, but there are more in a trusting look, in an extended hand, than in all that which keeps us from what we desire. And still, the world and men adorn all that which they oppose us with in order that we submit ourselves.

See this girl of the lean and straight chest — her head is an ardent cloud mingled with wings and claws. Down of flames and of steel. Her light eyes, her blue eyes are as heavy as black eyes.

On her fragile breaking skin no kiss would have the heart to attach itself.

This changing mouth follows all that it sees.

Man Ray draws so as not to forget himself, to be present, so that the world shall not disappear from his eyes. He draws to be loved.

Desire, life, are neither happy nor sad.

From the catalog of the exhibition, Valentin Gallery, New York, 1936   (Translated from the French)

Private Notes for and on Man Ray

Hans Richter 1966

Man Ray is a sorcerer. He has pulled more rabbits out of his beret than anyone before him, including his anti-art Dada friends Duchamp and Picabia. His art was never anti-art, but always anti-pretention, and so is he himself. Whenever I see him (and I see him for dinner always the first evening I arrive in Paris) I get the same quiet and reserved — enthusiastic welcome. That is the level on which our long friendship of forty years has established itself.

He is always the same unobtrusively — pessimistic optimist who can handle life, women, finances, art dealers, American businessmen, and visiting firemen just as expertly as he does photography and painting. He changes everything and everybody to suit his mood. There is no eggshell, no thermometer or metronome, no brick, bread or broom that he cannot and does not change into something else. It is as if he discovers the soul of each conventional object by liberating it from its practical function.

I have looked at hundreds of such strange objects in Paris, New York and Hollywood in his studio. They seemed to be born without the slightest effort as if each of them has created itself . . . without his moving a finger. It is the eye and this curious mind of his that creates them. Just by looking at them they reveal to him their poetic satus. All he has to do is to call the object by its true name.

Several years ago I saw an obviously very old manuscript, greyed by dust and years, lying in the corner of his studio. An old quill was still sticking to it. I grabbed the frail thing, but my hand got stuck in mid-air. Man Ray had tricked my vision. It weighed about four kilo, a folded piece of lead. He inscribed it for me with its true name "featherweight."

It accompanied me a long time in spite of its weight but I left it finally with other things at a friend's house in Ronco, Switzerland to collect it after my return. Amazingly enough somebody had stolen it. I hope whoever it was, understands its beauty. I loved it.

Looking back to those years of Dada, to the late tens and early twenties, I still remember how overwhelmed we were by our disgust with what other people called rationality, this vice on which people around us were thriving. To loosen its grip, to contradict it in life, art and ourselves, we separated ourselves with gusto from our so-called contemporaries. This disassociation gave us an unlimited freedom to discover new ways and to change the aspects of the world around us. We did not have to call a spade a spade anymore but made it an eye-opener, for which Duchamp used a coalshovel and for which Man Ray attached a melancholic eye on the pendulum of his metronome. His own, normally slightly melancholic eyes, do not express this "unwarranted optimism" of which he accuses me, but a slightly pessimistic expectancy. Also in life he does not trust the obvious. The fact that things are accepted by everybody does not convince him. He was already a famous fashion and portrait photographer in the twenties and no pretty woman or socially improtant beauty left Paris without being photographed by him. I would not say that he did not like that. But what bothered him besides pretty women and making a living was what photography really would look like on the other side of the moon and how he could reveal its hidden soul. The battle that Alfred Stieglitz had opened in the nineties of the last century, whether photography was an art and what it really could do, had long been joined by Man. He conquered it. As simple as all his transformations of the conventional into the poetic was his discovery of photography without a camera. The object was placed directly on the photographic plate or on film and developed: Ray-o-gram. That he discovered it seemed accidental. But then everything is. It is accidental that we are here, it is accidental that Man Ray is an inventor. He just cannot help to discover and reveal things because his whole person is involved in a process of continuous probing, of a natural distrust in things "being so."

He is methodical. In the twenties we were often eating together at the then favorite restaurant of the Surrealists, rue de Seine. To choose something to eat seemed for Man a process of complicated considerations. He pronounced that one should never eat (as 49 million Frenchman do) bread and meat at the same meal: "They have made experiments in the United States that prove conclusively that bread eaten with meat will ferment in the stomach and will prevent digestion." He explained in such clinical details that it took my appetite away. The fact that I would become sick bothered me less than the too detailed information of the juices working in my stomach while the waiter was serving my dinner. I reminded him lately of this theory of his. He shrugged it off and eats bread and meat at the same meal as if he had never consulted a health-horoscope. To the contrary, today he eats many things that in my opinion do not fit together. "It's all adaption," he explains, "like in marriage."

The funny thing is that the beginning of our relationship seemed to indicate anything else but a lasting friendship. It was about 1925. I was sitting on New Year's Eve with my girl-friend in the "Boeuf sur le toit," not especially expecting or begging for company ... when Man Ray showed up shortly before midnight. As the church bells introduced the New Year all the lights, politely, went off. I tried to kiss my girl at this appropriate occasion but could not find her. Only when the lights went on again I discovered her, not where I had wanted her to be, but in Man's arms. I must admit that this change disturbed me and it took the girl some time and effort to convince me of her honorable intentions (were they?). What I understood only much later though was the fact that destiny had sent Man especially as a saviour.

Had I only grasped its divine intentions I would have fled immediately and definitely; I would have gone to the next church to light the biggest candle.

More than twenty years later when my film *Dreams That Money Can Buy* had its opening at the Esquire Theater in Hollywood no trace of mutual mistrust could be found. To the contrary, he gave a big party for me decorated with pretty women and weighty men like Jean Renoir and Fritz Lang. In this way he was confirming not only our mutual esteem but also his approval of the episode "Ruth, Roses and Revolvers" which I had made after his story and included in *Dreams*. He himself appeared at its end as a bearded Man, burning fiercely to the sound of the carmagnole (adapted by Darius Milhaud).

I stayed in his little house and listened nightly fascinated to the song of the mocking-bird and daily to Man's impassionate discourses about the poetic variations which he imposed upon geometrical bodies on big canvases ...'til Juliette, in her soundless grace cooked the dinner.

Not in every corner of the world grow trees as green and full of fruits as Man. In spite of living half of his life in Paris one still can discover the glow of Philadelphia oscillating around his head. Of course he is now Parisian, but where would the "School of Paris" be without the contribution of foreigners ... creating the "School of Paris." He is part of it as he is of the schools of New York and Hollywood and all the others which sometimes copy and imitate him or develop his innovations further. He accepts both because he is Man Ray. Written for this catalog

Featherweight, 1960
Mixed media object
Collection Frida and Hans Richter, Southbury,
Connecticut
(Location unknown)

Frames from
Emak Bakia,
1926
Motion Picture

42

The Film Poetry of Man Ray

Carl I. Belz

Certain artists have a way of shifting their interests, of alternating between one medium and another, but also of making significant contributions to each one. Students of separate but related disciplines often concentrate upon only one sphere of activity and overlook the work in other areas. The general public frequently remains unaware of large sections of an individual's complete *oeuvre*. Some of these men — Marcel Duchamp, until recently, offers a case in point — are shuffled into a seemingly appropriate historical category and by many are thought to be inactive or no longer living. Similar distinctions apply to the American-born painter and photographer, Man Ray. Now 74, Ray remains active and has recently completed his autobiography.[1] Since 1910 he has jumped from one form of expression to another, and his works include not only painting and photography, but sculpture, collage, assemblage objects, writing and motion pictures as well. The recent influx within the commercial cinema of ideas which might formerly have been considered "experimental" brings into new relevance Ray's efforts in this medium, and it is with his films, and their relationship to poetry and literature of the nineteen-twenties that the present discussion is concerned.

Ray's involvements with the film medium are limited in number. On three occasions he contributed to projects conceived by other artists: Marcel Duchamp's *Anemic Cinema*, a study of revolving discs begun around 1920 and completed in Paris in 1926;[2] a Surrealist collaboration, *Essai de simulation de délire cinematographique*, with André Breton and Paul Éluard, initiated in the summer of 1935 but never completed;[3] and most recently a scenario entitled "Ruth, Roses and Revolvers" which was included in Hans Richter's *Dreams that Money Can Buy*, produced between 1944

and 1946. Ray's own films are four in number. The first of these, *Le Retour à la raison*, was an overnight production for a Dada show, *La Coeur à barbe*, which was organized by Tristan Tzara in 1923. Tzara, one of the Dada leaders, had listed in the announcement of the soiree that a film by Man Ray would be screened, but Ray himself had not been informed about his contribuition. When Tzara did tell him — the day before the show — Ray felt it would make a good Dada joke since no such film existed. But Tzara insisted, pointing out that since Ray made photographs without a camera — his well-known Rayographs — he could certainly produce films in the same manner; Ray consented and within twenty-four hours completed a short work to conclude the program. The film, unfortunately lost, apparently scored a Dada success, not only because of its extraordinary conception via the photogram technique, but also because the makeshift splices broke apart several times during the showing.[4]

Three films of related character followed *Le Retour à la raison*: *Emak Bakia* in 1926, *L'Etoile de mer* in 1928, and *Les Mysteres du Chateau du dé* in 1929. All, of course, were silent shorts, though a musical accompaniment was intended for each one, selected by the artist, and generally consisting of contemporary jazz or popular music. Each was largely a one-man project, that is, filmed and directly by Ray himself, though assistant cameramen worked on the latter two.[5] *L'Etoile de mer* was the only film to have a scenario of any kind, being based upon a short unpublished

[1] *Self Portrait,* Boston, Atlantic-Little, Brown, 1963.
[2] For this collaboration, see Robert Lebel, *Marcel Duchamp,* New York, Grove Press, 1959, pp. 51—2.
[3] Interview with the artist, Paris, April, 1962; for stills of the material which was completed, see *Cahiers d'art,* vol. 10, nos. 5—6, 1935, p. 107.
[4] Interview; also see A. Kyrou, *Le Surrealism au Cinema,* Arcanes, 1953, p. 177, and A. Knight, *The Liveliest Art,* New York, 1957, pp. 101—2.
[5] Interview; Kyrou, *op. cit.,* p. 180, mentions Boiffard as the operator for *Les Mystères.*

Le Beau Temps,
1939
Oil
112×108″
Collection Mr. and
Mrs. Man Ray,
Paris   44

poem by Robert Desnos which Ray admits having followed very closely.[6] The last film in this group resulted from an idea proposed by the French patron of the arts, the Vicomte de Noailles. It centers upon the Vicomte's villa in Southern France, an international style building designed by Mallet-Stevens. None of the films were commercial projects, and none were so ambitious as to require professional actors or actresses. About the most "famous" personality to appear was the model "Kiki" who took a role in *L'Etoile de mer.* For *Les Mysteres du Chateau du dé* Ray simply used as characters the Vicomte's weekend guests and concealed their identities with blank stocking masks.[7]

French film, during the decade of the 'twenties, is usually referred to as the "avant-garde cinema."[8] As an art form the motion picture at that time was still relatively unexplored. Many of the techniques which today are taken for granted were then in an undeveloped or undiscovered state. As they were discovered new methods often became ends in themselves. Thus Jacques Brunius complains that the majority of films produced in France between 1920 and 1925 suffered from an overdose of rapid cutting, superimpositions, the crick-necked camera, and photographic distortions.[9] In his three existing films from the 1920's Man Ray employs similar and related techniques to those mentioned by Brunius. However, like the master film makers of the period — René Clair for instance — the artist does not permit camera technique to dominate his work. Each of the films produces a different series of visual effects, and in each one technique serves to enhance rather than dictate the cinema aesthetic. If one element may be considered common to all three, it is a quality which Ray himself calls "poetry."[10] One intention of his film ideas he describes as causing the spectator, after viewing a picture, "to rush out and breathe the pure air of the outside, be a leading actor and solve his own dramatic problems. In that way he would realize a long cherished dream of becoming a poet, an artist himself, instead of being merely a spectator. Poets have declared that everyone should write poetry. All art is the writing of poetry and the painting of pictures."[11] Ray's films seem to constitute his personal "writing of poetry." In the following discussion we shall attempt to demonstrate this point, at the same time clarifying the term in its relationship to the film in general and to Surrealism, the movement to which this cinema makes an important contribution.

Emak Bakia represents a development of the ideas contained in *Le Retour à la raison.* About half of the picture consists of abstract images, some of which are film Rayographs similar to those in the 1923 Dada production. However, the majority of non-objective images are light reflection — that is, forms produced by bouncing lights off lustrous metallic surfaces or through glass prisms. Such forms do not immediately reveal their origin. At times they appear like water reflections though in other moments the vague shapes seem to result from the multiple intersections of moving beams of light. Generally these abstractions are alternated with representational sequences: cars, peoples, landscapes, and still life objects.

Ray describes the character of his film in the following way: "A series of fragments, a cine-poem with a certain optical sequence make up a whole that still remains a fragment. Just as one can much better appreciate the abstract beauty in the essentials in cine-

[6] Interview.

[7] After completing *Les Mystères*, Ray was asked by the Vicomte to do a full length film, a commercial venture. However, Ray declined the opportunity, and the patronage went to Cocteau for *La Sang d'un poète* and Bunuel for *L'Age d'or* (Interview; also Kyrou, *op. cit.,* p. 181).

[8] See, for example, S. Kracauer, *Theory of Film,* New York, 1960, pp. 339—49.

[9] "Experimental Film in France," in R. Manvell, ed., *Experiment in the Film,* London, 1949, pp. 84—5.

[10] Interview.

[11] Frank Stauffacher, ed., *Art in Cinema,* San Francisco, 1947, p. 26.

matography. It is not an 'abstract' film or a story-teller; its reasons for being are its inventions of light forms and movements, while the more objective parts interrupt the monotony of abstract inventions or serve as punctuation."[12]

Ray's statement mentions a "certain optical sequence," although it does not clarify the nature of this sequence. The remarks further suggest a random juxtaposition of indentifiable and abstract images, the former, by implication, might be thought to occupy a position of lesser significance — within the total aesthetic — that of punctuation — than the latter. The experience of the film, however, indicates otherwise — namely that representation and abstraction are related in such a manner as to reveal fundamental qualities common to both. Early in the picture, for example, a sequence of Rayographs is presented. The shadows of miniature objects (tacks, buttons, grains of salt, although none are immediately identifiable) dance across the screen. Moments later the moving lights of a night-time news marquee are seen. The two sets of images are based upon similar visual components: small white forms which flash across a dark and cloudy background. The pair of sequences, as a result of a carefully selected method of presenting the objects' respective abstract qualities, equates objective and non-objective realities.

The interplay recurs in other parts of the film. Another sequence opens with a night scene of the ocean, and shows waves gently lapping a deserted beach. As the camera nears the water it rotates to an inverted position, eliminating the beach and horizon, and picturing only the flowing surface of the sea. The abstract movements have a strong resemblance to the light reflections which appear earlier in the film. Once again a visually objective scene is distilled for its abstract elements. The latter sequence is followed by a "fish section"; actual fish are photographed, but a

series of superimpositions emphasizes the fluid quality of marine life and the creatures' natural movements.

The film does not consist only of these nature-abstraction comparisons. Certain parts have a distinctly Dadaist flavor. When a car which we have watched as it cruises through the country comes to rest, an extraordinary number of people emerge. We see only their feet as they descend on to the running board. As with the "fish section," the visual joke is achieved through superimposed shots of a single person climbing from the automobile. In another representational sequence of *Emak Bakia* an expensive convertible car stops before a house. A man emerges, carrying a valise, and proceeds into the building. Once inside his room he tears the collar from his shirt and casts it to the floor. He then opens the valise. It is filled with white collars which, one by one, he tears and throws to the floor. About this time, however, the collars begin to rotate. As their animations accelerate they tend to move out of focus. A series of fluid, non-objective forms results, and it is gradually fused with the water-like movements and reflections reminiscent of preceding images in the film. With this scene Ray produces a kind of "readymade-for-the-film" situation. Commonplace obejcts are removed from their ordinary environment, and their original function is in this manner denied. Their place within the total film bears no narrative or logical associations. It is the shift of environment which counts, for this displacement releases the object's abstract or artistic potential.

With scenes like the ones discussed above, the poetic character of *Emak Bakia* emerges. As Ray says, the film consists of a number of fragments. The relationships among them, however, are not of a progressive nature. No story is presented, nor is there a visual or purely artistic conclusion. The individual optical sequences stimulate intellectual paradoxes and relationships: real and unreal, objective and non-objective, abstraction and representation. Inanimate objects

[12] *Ibid.,* p. 53.

come to life, shadows dance, and we see fish whose movements, like those in Klee's *Fish Magic,* seem more "fish-like" than their counterparts in nature. But the images are never presented in a logical fashion. With each cut the viewer finds himself in a new environment: at first in an abstract world, then in the open country, a house, at the beach, under water and so forth. One can never predict the coming vision, whether it will be of a non-objective realm or some familiar and commonplace surroundings. The film's poetic quality resides in its use of sequences which function like independent words or clauses within a general stream of images. Of course such poetry has a very special cast. Aptly characterized by its "play of the free spirit,"[13] it is best exemplified by men like Philippe Soupault, Max Jacob, Jean Cocteau or Paul Eluard, to name only a few of the many individuals already active betwen World War I and the official declaration of Surrealism by André Breton in 1924. The guiding aesthetic of such poetry is difficult to isolate. Like so much of what we call Dada in literature or the visual arts, it consists of an elusive and random mixture of joy and disgust, acceptance and negation, the concrete and fantastic. According to Marcel Raymond, its special quality "can be detected in unusual conjunctures — it is an occult relation between seemingly unrelated events, a concatenation of unacknowledged circumstances, an association of images produced by some demon of analogy, defying all reason. The poem does not trace the concentric circles of the dancer whose figures bring him back to his starting point; it is animated by an internal dynamism, it presents acts, facts. However, it moves on a plane which is not that of everyday life nor quite that of a dream; it subsists in an intermediate zone, half way between the real and unreal (or what is called the unreal), the land of enchantments, of certain forms of mystification, and of the modern fantastic."[14]

Such, for example, is the nature of Cocteau's *Dos d'Ange*:

A false street in a dream
And this unreal piston
Are lies fomented
By an angel from heaven.

Whether it be a dream or not a dream,
When you look at it from above
You discover the lie,
Because the angels are hunchbacked.

At least their shadow
On the wall of my room is hunchbacked.[15]

Or these lines by Philippe Soupault:

The airplane weaves telegraphic wires
And the fountain sings the same song
At the coachmen's rendevous the aperitif is
   orange-colored
But the locomotive mechanics have white eyes
The lady has lost her smile in the woods.[16]

Ray's film exhibits the same free-wheeling spirit. Reality is present, but it is surrounded with the aura of fantasy. The motion picture camera captures what Paul Eluard calls the "fugitive relationship between things": momentary sequences which have no logical destination except to stimulate a sense of the marvelous. The latter quality is basic to the aesthetic of *Emak Bakia*. As a total entity it possibly exhibits less mystery or enchantment than do the majority of proto-Surrealist expressions. But it shares with them the ability to equate that which would ordinarily seem to defy comparison, to remove objects from their common environment, and to see in the commonplace something marvelous and visionary. It constitutes a

[13] Marcel Raymond, *From Baudelaire to Surrealism,* New York, 1949, pp. 252—69.
[14] *Ibid.,* p. 259.
[15] Translated in Raymond, p. 259—60.
[16] Translated in Raymond, p. 279—80.

way of seeing rather than a pointed statement about reality, and in this manner avoids the utilitarianism anathematized by Surrealist theory.

With *L'Etoile de mer* Ray's poetic sensibilities are more obvious since the film closely follows the verse of Robert Desnos. Georges Lemaitre has summarized Desnos' poetry in the following manner: "The works ... mirror the supreme Surrealist entity as viewed from the focal point of love. One would search vainly in them, however, for the metaphysical quality which characterizes most of Eluard's productions. Desnos seems to wallow with special predilection in the repulsive quagmire of physical eroticism. There livid, slimy forms of sensual perversity, aroused from their heavy slumber, twist and turn ignominously, releasing in their convulsive spasms an acrid and suffocating stench. The spectacle is not devoid, it must be said, of a certain awesome grandeur."[17] The following quatrains from "La Liberté ou l'Amour," while largely avoiding the "repulsive quagmire of physical eroticism," do capture Desnos' sense of emotional excess and delirium, qualities which are clearly expressed by Ray's film:

... It's in a clean café with unpolished mirrors
That we treated humanity like a puppet theater
Past people, future people, canceled visions,
And aspects of the word in holy trinity.

At times we catch our hands tracing flowers
On steamy panes of glass while, on the river,
Mighty trawlers go down toward the ports
And the bridge pilings put on new robes.

We dare not recall our drowning vows
Up in arms and to finish with these swine,
Men, we like make-up and glances,
Then we mimick love with frightful raptures.

Girls' eyes are knots at our wrists,
What reason is there to love so many faces?

What are we waiting for? It is the hour when fritters
 are singing.
Our eyes will burst at the rose corsages ...

... And since then we search the dull and cloudy night
Hoping that before dawn in that deserted sky,
Lighting up at each stroke, a swimmer
Will reconcile love and liberty.[18]

The fluency of this verse is similar to the rhythm of Ray's film. Each sequence in *L'Etoile de mer* is an independent unit, and the relationship between the segments is, for the most part, only tenuously maintained. Although love and eroticism constitute the basic themes of the picture, it is, like the earlier *Emak Bakia*, without narrative or climax. A couple meets on the street and we follow them to the girl's apartment. We see them caress; we see her dressed and undressed, in and out of bed. But these more sensuous moments are constantly interspersed with other images: the deserted street, the roof tops, an empty field, the sea, a still life, or a trash can and a stack of discarded newspapers. These contrasts are accompanied at times by touches of humor: with the lover seated beside her, a woman slowly undresses and steps into bed; the man arises and they bid farewell. Or: an intimate-looking couple walks along a quiet street; as a second gentleman approaches, the woman, without comment, goes off with him.

If love, eroticism and woman provide the essence of the film, they are certainly not idealized. There is, in other words, much of Desnos' use of abrupt and sensuous contrasts. The film thus exhibits a certain deceptive character. Along with scenes of the softest sensuosity, the more blatant and obscene image of

[17] G. Lemaitre, *From Cubism to Surrealism in French Literature*, Cambridge, 1941, p. 211.
[18] I would like to thank Dr. Paul Mankin of the Department of Romance Languages, University of Massachusetts, for his translation of this poem which is published in Rosa Buchole's *L'Évolution Poetique de Robert Desnos*, Brussels, 1956, p. 106.

the star fish constantly reappears with its wreathing tentacles, scaly surface, and ugly, devouring mouth. Different sequences emphasize the opposition of the female with the sea creature, and employ submarine imagery which is typical of a large number of Surrealist pictorial expressions during this period. Here one need only recall the paintings of Miro, Masson or Tanguy, all of which utilize fluid froms and water-like backgrounds in order to heighten an atmosphere of mystery and enchantment. In an example from the film, the woman, whom we have seen resting upon her bed, begins to rise. The camera follows her leg as it emerges from the soft linen and alights on the floor. But on the floor, and immediately before her foot, lies the repulsive star fish. One can hardly avoid the visual conclusion, the comparison of the love object with the beast consisting solely of arms or legs.

The steady interplay of opposing elements, of the attractive with the repulsive, produces a love poem with distinctly sordid overtones. The paradox is enhanced by the style of the pictures, many of which are filmed through a pane of distorting glass. Scenes realized in this manner have a softness and atmospheric quality which is reminiscent of Impressionist paintings. The dreamy veil which this technique casts over much of *L'Etoile de mer* adds to the idealist half of the two-sided overtones. The occasional scenes in clear focus, however, serve as stylistic reminders that the purist ideal can be presented from another point of view — perhaps less inviting, but possibly more factual. The attraction-repulsion combination is a typical Surrealist device, and the female has often been the target for some Sadistic or provocative blend of images. The device recurs throughout Surrealist works of art: in Man Ray's solarization photograph, *The Primacy of Mind over Matter*, where a woman's naked body seems to melt and flow upon the floor; in Magritte's *The Rape*, where the unadorned torso has been transplanted, point for point, for the woman's face. In Surrealist or quasi-Surrealist films similar devices ap-

Scene from *Les Mysteres du Chateau de dé*
Movie

pear. *Un Chien Andalou* is an obvious example, and Bunuel does not seem to have lost his penchant for lusty provocation: in his recent *Viridiana* the famous director places a young and attractive religious novice in the company of thieves, beggars, and a typical entourage of social outcasts, and then proceeds to symbolize a general degeneracy by the details of the girl's personal downfall.

Both *Emak Bakia* and *L'Etoile de mer*, of course, were silent productions. For both, however, the artist has designated that they can be given sound accompaniments, even though neither demands a sound track to reveal dialogue or environmental noises. Even in *L'Etoile de mer*, where people confront one another, it is their action and movement and, therefore, the image which dominates. For both films we have suggestions by Ray regarding the type of music he prefers for their accompaniment. In the case of *Emak Bakia* he designates old jazz, though "any collection of old jazz will do."[19] For *L'Etoile de mer* the artist

[19] P. Velguth, "Notes on the musical accompaniment to the silent films," in Stauffacher, ed., *op., cit.,* pp. 91—5.

prefers popular French music.[20] Along with these specific designations, a statement by Hans Richter enables us to generalize Ray's theories of sound accompaniment: "I agree with Man Ray that we must avoid complete synchronization. We should find a way to let the sound and the picture move on its own in the same direction, but nevertheless, separately. This refers to the spoken word as well as the musical or other sounds."[21] Thus in *Emak Bakia*, for instance, the quick tempo of the jazz sounds provides an aural parallel for the staccato editing, the dancing rhythms of the non-objective Rayographs, and scenes from a speeding automobile. In addition, the improvisatory quality of the music harmonizes with the abstract nature of the flowing acquatic forms and the prismatic reflections. By avoiding complete synchronization of sound and image, Ray maintains the fragmentary and impromptu character of the film. Visually, the picture, with its changing rhythms, techniques and subjects, possesses the segmented and unpredictable quality of "free spirit" poetry. The presence of music having a similarly spontaneaus nature therefore enhances visual aesthetic.

This theory for the cinematic use of musical accompaniment seems to have been typical of the avant-garde film makers of the 1920's. As noted, the above quote applies to Hans Richter and Man Ray. Richter also explains that for his own early film, *Rhythmus 21,* and for Eggling's *Diagonal Symphony*, he plays Bach.[22] Considering the environment from which these films emerged, we could probably have anticipated such a theory, even though three decades of sound film may now cause us to think only of its experimental character. In the silent era the majority or these films were conceived in purely visual terms, and the question of their musical accompaniment, therefore, must have occured largely as an afterthought. With a completed film then, the easiest and most logical way to accompany it and still, as Richter says, "let the sound and the picture move on its own in the same direction,"

would be to adopt a similarly independent but finished score. Such a method would almost automatically insure a degree of asynchronomy. The major task was to find music whose *character* would parallel the film, a general prerequisite which seems to have been easily satisfied by selecting from the vast range of Bach to Stravinsky.[23]

Man Ray's third film from the decade of the 1920's, *Les Mysteres du Chateau du dé*, is in some respects comparable to the two we have been discussing. As in the earlier films Ray utilizes a full repertory of camera techniques in order to achieve a multiplicity of visual effects. Reflected shots, dissolves, slow and reverse motion are all included in this category. And like the other pictures, *Les Mysteres* presents no logical or developed story line, nor is there any visual or narrative conclusion. In the latter respect, however, this film is perhaps the most deceptive of the three. For, superficially, it bears all the trademarks of the objective story-telling cinema. At the beginning of the film two people are seen in a café. They leave, get into a car, and begin an all-night drive, arriving in daylight at a country town. They approach a villa, the nature and planning of which are scrupulously investigated by the camera as the explorers traverse both its exterior and interior. Other characters are then introduced, and we see them seated together on the lawn, swimming, exercising, sleeping. Nearly all of these actions seem clear, and generally their sequence ap-

[20] *Ibid.*   [21] *Ibid.*   [22] *Ibid.*

[23] *Ibid.*, for the complete list of musical accompaniments used in the San Francisco symposium. The employment of a pre-existing score was not the only method of obtaining an asynchronous musical accompaniment, nor were Ray and Richter the only adherents of the principle. Russian film makers, namely Eisenstein, Pudovkin, and Alexandrov, also proposed an asynchronous theory. In the case of Potemkin music was composed after the completion of the film to fulfill this theory. For the Russian statement of the problem, see S. Eisenstein, *Film Form,* trans. and ed. by J. Leyda, New York, 1957, pp. 257–60.

pears logical and ordinary enough. But it is in this seeming logicality, this "lure" of reality, that the deception and "surreality" of the film is revealed.

On an artistic level this Surrealistic character deserves consideration. In both content and style the film is comparable to a large body of Surrealist painting. The painting to which we refer may be considered under the general heading of "objective" or "representational." It is the type of work found frequently in René Magritte, Paul Delvaux, the early de Chirico, often in Salvador Dali, and occasionally in Max Ernst. A precisionist technique also seems characteristic of much of this painting. Magritte's *The Human Condition* is a good example. The subject matter of this picture — at least the objects which it depicts — is immediately recognizable: the wall of a room, a window, curtains, an easel, a landscape. Only upon second glance, when the extraordinary fusion of the easel and the landscape becomes clear, does the viewer realize that the superficial reality is but a spring-board for a world of ideas. The early de Chirico cityscapes, filled by the tension of a quiet lonely atmosphere, provide a similar experience.

Ray's *Mysteres* establishes a world that is comparable to the paintings mentioned above. There is in it the same "apparent" reality of buildings, landscapes, people and their actions. Again, however, the reality is deceptive. In the first half of the villa sequence only the building itself is seen; both the visitors and the supposed inhabitants are out of sight. As the camera scans the deserted gardens, the stark concrete walls, and then the unpopulated interior rooms, an atmosphere of suspense develops, one which seems almost like a parody of some mystery thriller. The type of atmosphere, however, seems to place the film more in a Surrealist context than of the mock detective adventure. The stillness, the shadows, and the cold architectural forms all help to set a de Chirico-like stage, and the visual experience is like moving through a sequence of the master's mysterious and paradoxical paintings. Even where characters appear the tension is maintained. Each person wears a mask which completely covers his or her face.

Before long certain disturbing details begin to shatter any illusion of reality. Seated on the lawn, the guests throw enormous dice. While exercising, they toss a ball which suddenly moves of its own accord. The characters' movements, as they swim and play, have a strange, artificial quality. Together these elements increase the mysterious aspect of the cinematic presentation. It appears, in fact, that some cult rites are being enacted before our eyes, an impression which is intensified when, at one point, the "initiates" dissolve after concluding their "exercises." As the nature of these details becomes more obvious, we realize that the normality of the world in and around the chateau is only an apparent one. What happens thus seems dream-like in essence, and the "real" becomes transformed into the "surreal."

Comparisons with painting are not the only ones which help shed light on the nature of Ray's film. With *Emak Bakia* and *L'Etoile de mer* we also considered poetry, pointing out in both cases the disjointed and illogical sequences and their relevance to contemporary French verse. Ray's last film from this decade does not lend itself to the same type of comparison. There is in the picture too strong a narrative sense, albeit it one which, as we have tried to indicate, does not produce a conventional story or conclusion. If any literary comparison is possible it would seem to lie more in the medium of prose than poetry. Certain works of the period do seem to embody the type of Surrealist expression which we found in the 1929 film. In *The Art of Assemblage*, William Seitz selects André Gide as being exemplary of the modernism of literature in the 1920's. He writes, "For *The Counterfeiters* (*Les Faux-Monnayeurs*, 1925), Gide worked out a method, intentionally dispersive, from his earlier work on the structure of the novel. He replaced traditional narration by a coreless sequence of events and data strung together almost without a common theme"; and further, "By dissociation, by refusing to resolve disparate elements, he retains an openness more typical of life than of art."[24] Within the circle of Ray's immediate acquaintances, the writings of Jean Cocteau or Philippe Soupault deserve mention in the same context. Cocteau's *Les Enfants Terribles*, especially in the opening sequences of the schoolboys' snowball fight, reveals some of the subterranean fantasies which dominate children's lives. An event of apparent levity and good feelings is thus shown to contain a world of seething emotional anxieties and enchantments. Cocteau's novel dates from 1930, just one year after the completion of Ray's picture. Soupault's *Dernieres Nuits des Paris* was published in the same year that the film appeared, 1929. Its affinity to *Les Mysteres* is even closer than is the Cocteau novel which ultimately depicts a sphere quite alien to that of the country villa. Soupault does not concentrate on the same personages as Ray, but rather involves himself with thieves and prostitutes. Common to the film and the novel, however, is their mutual aura of mystery and expectation and the corresponding lack of any explicitly revealing action. Things happen — there is a murder, a search, the killer is eventually revealed, the narrator encounters various Parisian characters — but, in the traditional sense, no plot or resolution unifies the events. More important seems to be the ambiguity, the uncertainty, and the mystery surrounding a world whose *dramatis personae* — a whore, a sailor, a dog, and their respective friends — would superficially seem clear and direct. But instead of clarity, the explicit idea of "not knowing," of being unable to understand these people or their actions, seems to be emphasized. All of Soupault's action takes place at night; he seems, in fact, to stress the daylight as being frightening because it might reveal unwanted truth and reality. Georgette, the prostitute, is described as being a virtual incarnation of the night; as one character says, "Tell me, when Georgette disappears, have you noticed that day is not far distant? If she should disappear forever, I have a feeling, and believe me I don't let things muddle me, I have a feeling there would be no more night." Later, when the girl returns home at dawn, we note that "day splashed the casing of the stairs, and all the blemishes wrought by time appeared." An additional feature of uncertainty is provided by the character Volpe, a diletante columinst, who constantly reminds the narrator, when the latter remarks about Georgette or some other person, "you hardly know them," or simply, "you don't know them at all."

Similar to Ray's characters, those in Soupault's novel seem to wear masks. We see them in action, but we know nothing about them. Once again we have a paradoxical, dream-like reality. We are lured into a special world where recognizable forms lead a double existence. The ambiguity of Ray's prose-poetry film world, or of Soupault's novel, seems characteristic of Surrealist expression in general, of that kind of double imagery we find in Dali or Magritte paintings. And in all cases — film, novel or painting — the artistic emphasis is upon unknown rather than apparent realities.

To isolate these literary or cinematic phenomena in the decade of the 'twenties is not, of course, completely valid. Both French and Italian films of recent years — the work, for instance, of Resnais, Truffaut, or Antonioni — have brought to the once well-defined "commercial" screen new statements regarding space and time, statements which were formerly typed "art house experiments." Neither does recent cinema respect the limitations of conventional narrative and plot sequence. As we see more of this work we begin to realize that the French *avant-garde* was not just a playful experiment itself. The films of the 'twenties are becoming freshly and increasingly relevant; and to the cinema prophecies of that era belong the works of Man Ray.   From *Criticism*, a quarterly of literature and the arts, Spring 1965.

[24] W. Seitz, *The Art of Assemblage*, New York, 1961, p. 17.

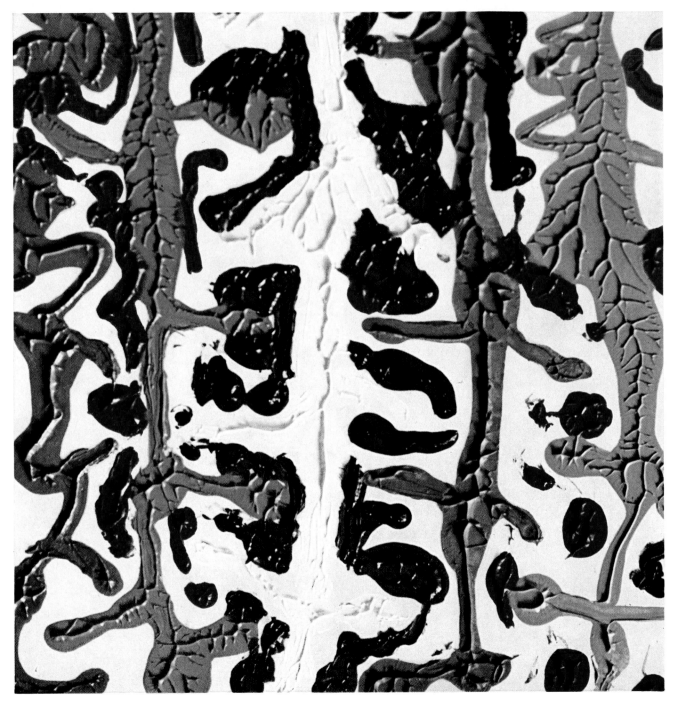

53

Peinte Naturelle, 1958
Oil   14 x 17″
Collection Mr. and Mrs. Albert Lewin, New York

Catalog of the Exhibition

* illustrated

PAINTINGS

1. *Figures in Landscape*, c. 1908
   Oil
   14 x 24"
   Lent by Mr. and Mrs. David Savage

*2. *Dual Portrait*, 1913
   Oil
   12¹/₂ x 10¹/₂"
   Lent by Mr. and Mrs. Man Ray

*3. *The Village*, 1913
   Oil
   20 x 16"
   Lent by Mr. and Mrs. Albert Lewin

*4. *Woman Asleep*, 1913
   Oil
   12 x 16"
   Lent by Whitney Museum of
   American Art,
   Gift of Mrs. Katharine Kuh

5. *Portrait of Alfred Stieglitz*, 1913
   Oil
   10¹/₂ x 8¹/₂"
   Lent by Yale University Library,
   Alfred Stieglitz Archives

*6. *Untitled*, 1914
   Ink and wash
   7¹/₂ x 9¹/₂"
   Collection Los Angeles County
   Museum of Art,
   Gift of Mrs. Florence Homolka

*7. *Five Figures*, 1914
   Oil
   36 x 32"
   Lent by Whitney Museum of
   American Art,
   Gift of Mrs. Katharine Kuh

*8. *A.D. MCMXIV*, 1914
   Oil
   36¹/₂ x 68¹/₂"
   Lent by Philadelphia Museum
   of Art, A. E. Gallatin Collection

*9. *Ramapo*, 1914
   Oil
   20 x 19"
   Lent by Cordier & Ekstrom, Inc.

*10. *Man Ray, 1914*, 1914
   Oil
   7 x 5"
   Lent by Sir Roland and
   Lady Penrose

11. *The Reaper*, 1914
   Oil
   26 x 38"
   Lent by Mr. and Mrs. Man Ray

*12. *The Rug*, 1914
   Oil
   18¹/₂ x 20¹/₂"
   Lent by Mr. and Mrs. Man Ray

*13. *Departure of Summer*, 1914
   Oil
   33¹/₂ x 35¹/₂"
   Lent by P. N. Matisse Gallery

14. *Totem*, 1914
   Oil
   35¹/₂ x 23³/₄"
   Lent by P. N. Matisse Gallery

*15. *Arrangements of Form*, 1915
   Oil
   17¹/₂ x 11¹/₂"
   Lent by Cordier & Ekstrom, Inc.

16. *Grand Arrangement of Forms*, 1915
   Oil
   34¹/₂ x 32"
   Lent by Cordier & Ekstrom, Inc.

17. *Arrangement of Forms*, 1915
   Oil
   18 x 12"
   Lent by Mr. and Mrs. Man Ray

18. *Promenade*, 1915
   Oil
   24 x 19¹/₂"
   Lent by J. Daniel Weitzman

19. *Promenade*, 1915
   Oil
   42 x 34"
   Lent by Dr. and Mrs. Paul Wescher

20. *Promenade*, 1915
   Gouache
   10¹/₂ x 8¹/₄"
   Lent by Mr. and Mrs. Man Ray

*21. *Dance*, 1915
   Oil
   28 x 36"
   Lent Anonymously

22. *Black Widow*, 1916
   Oil
   72 x 36"
   Lent Anonymously

*23. *Orchestra*, 1916
   Oil
   52 x 36"
   Lent Anonymously

24. *Suicide*, 1917
Aerograph
23 1/2 x 18"
Lent by D. and J. de Menil

*25. *The Rope Dancer Accompanies Herself with Her Shadows*, 1917
Aerograph
13 3/8 x 17 3/8"
Lent by Mr. and Mrs. Morton G. Neumann

26. *La Volière*, 1919
Aerograph
28 x 22"
Lent by Sir Roland and Lady Penrose

27. *Admiration of the Orchestrelle for the Cinematograph*, 1919
Aerograph
26 x 21 1/2"
Lent by The Museum of Modern Art, Gift of A. Conger Goodyear

*28. *Hermaphrodite*, 1919
Aerograph
20 x 16 1/8"
Lent Anonymously

*29. *Untitled*, 1919
Aerograph
29 1/2 x 23 1/2"
Lent by Cordier & Ekstrom, Inc.

30. *Jazz*, 1919
Aerograph
27 1/4 x 21 1/4"
Lent by The Columbus Gallery of Fine Arts

*31. *Rrose Sélavy*, 1923
Oil
23 1/4 x 19 1/2"
Lent Anonymously

*32. *Kiki*, 1923
Oil
24 x 18"
Lent by Mr. and Mrs. David Savage

33. *Usine dans la Forêt*, 1929
Oil
25 1/2 x 32"
Lent by Mr. and Mrs. Man Ray

*34. *Gens du Monde*, 1929
Oil on gold leaf
78 3/4 x 39 3/8"
Lent by Mr. and Mrs. Albert Lewin

*35. *Gens d'Intérieur*, 1929
Oil on silver leaf
78 3/4 x 39 3/8"
Lent by Mr. and Mrs. Man Ray

*36. *Enemy Houses*, 1933
Oil
39 x 39"
Lent Anonymously

*37. *Observation Time — The Lovers*, 1932—34
Oil
39 3/8 x 98 1/2"
Lent Anonymously

38. *Return to Reason*, 1938
Oil
80 x 50"
Lent by Mr. and Mrs. Man Ray

39. *The Wall*, 1938
Oil
19 3/4 x 25 1/2"
Lent by Dr. and Mrs. Howard Taswell

*40. *The Misunderstood One*, 1938
Oil
24 x 18"
Lent by Mr. and Mrs. Man Ray

*41. *Imaginary Portrait of D. A. F. de Sade*, 1938
Oil
21 5/8 x 17 3/4"
Lent Anonymously

Chess Set, n.d.
Wood
Collection of Samuel Siegler, Teaneck, New Jersey

Tapestry, 1911
Mixed media object   65 x 45^1/$_2$"
Collection Mr. and Mrs. Man Ray, Paris

*42. *The Fortune*, 1938
Oil
23 x 28"
Lent by Mr. and Mrs. Edwin
Bergman

*43. *Easel Painting*, 1938
Oil
38 x 30"
Lent by Mr. and Mrs. Man Ray

*44. *The Woman and Her Fish*, 1938
Oil
23⅝ x 28¾"
Lent by The Trustees of
The Tate Gallery

*45. *Le Beau Temps*, 1939
Oil
112 x 108"
Lent by Mr. and Mrs. Man Ray

46. *Personnage*, 1939
Oil
Lent by Jacques Kaplan

47. *Trompe l'Œil*, 1939
Oil
19½ x 25½"
Lent by Mr. and Mrs. Thomas Kelly

*48. *Twins*, 1939
Oil
38 x 30"
Lent by Mr. and Mrs. Man Ray

*49. *Abstraction,* 1940
Oil
26 x 22"
Collection Los Angeles County
Museum of Art,
Gift of Dr. and Mrs. Paul Wescher

50. *The Poet*, 1941
Oil
16 x 20"
Lent by Dr. and Mrs. Howard
Taswell

51. *Leda and the Swan*, 1941
Oil
30 x 40"
Lent by Dr. and Mrs. Howard
Taswell

52. *Self-Portrait*, 1941
Oil
23¾ x 19½"
Lent by Joseph Hirshhorn

53. *Promenade*, 1941
Oil
60 x 40¼"
Lent by Yale University Art Gallery,
Collection Société Anonyme

REVOLVING DOORS
(series related to 1916—1917
collages, cat. nos. 54—63)

54. *Mime,* 1942
Oil
30 x 20"
Lent by Mr. and Mrs. Man Ray

55. *Long Distance*, 1942
Oil
30 x 20"
Lent by Mr. and Mrs. Man Ray

56. *Orchestra*, 1942
Oil
30 x 20"
Lent by Mr. and Mrs. Man Ray

57. *The Meeting*, 1942
Oil
30 x 20"
Lent by Mr. and Mrs. Man Ray

58. *Legend*, 1942
Oil
30 x 20"
Lent by Mr. and Mrs. Man Ray

59. *Decanter*, 1942
Oil
30 x 20"
Lent by Mr. and Mrs. Man Ray

60. *Young Girl*, 1942
Oil
30 x 20"
Lent by Mr. and Mrs. Man Ray

61. *Shadows*, 1942
Oil
30 x 20"
Lent by Mr. and Mrs. Man Ray

62. *Concrete Mixer*, 1942
Oil
30 x 20"
Lent by Mr. and Mrs. Man Ray

63. *Dragon Fly*, 1942
Oil
30 x 20"
Lent by Mr. and Mrs. Man Ray

*64. *Infinite Man*, 1942
Oil
72 x 50"
Lent by Mr. and Mrs. Man Ray

65. *L'Equivoque*, 1943
Oil
27 x 22"
Lent by Joseph Hirshhorn

66. *Two Figures and an Eagle.
A Picture with a Handle*, 1943
Oil
10½ x 30"
Lent by Mr. and Mrs. Bernard Reis

67. *Dream of a Key*, 1943
Oil
51 x 25"
Lent by Mr. and Mrs.
George Rosenthal

68. *Cactus*, 1945
Oil
18¼ x 24"
Lent by Mr. and Mrs. Man Ray

69. *Cactus*, 1945
Oil
38 x 30"
Lent by Sir Roland and
Lady Penrose

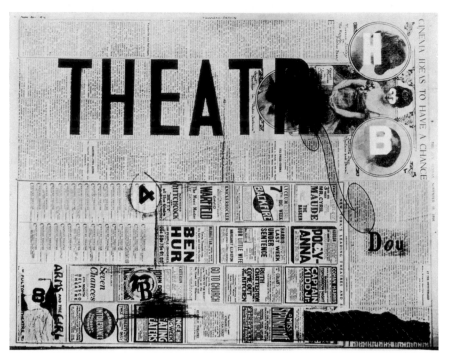

Theatr, 1916
Collage   18 x 24″
Coll. Moderna Museet, Stockholm

78. *Julius Caesar*, 1948
Oil
24 x 19³/₄″
Lent by Mr. and Mrs. Melvin Jacobs

*79. *Midsummer Night's Dream*, c. 1948
Oil
25 x 31″
Lent by Mr. and Mrs.
Herbert Kendall

*80. *Merry Wives of Windsor*, 1948
Oil
24 x 18″
Lent by Cordier & Ekstrom, Inc.

81. *Othello*, c. 1948
Oil
Lent by Mme. Simone Colinet

82. *Taming of the Shrew*, c. 1948
Oil
15¹/₂ x 19″
Lent by Mr. and Mrs. Albert Lewin

83. *Anthony and Cleopatra*, c. 1948
Oil
Lent by Claude Hersaint

84. *Merchant of Venice*, c. 1948
Oil
29³/₄ x 39³/₄″
Lent by Mr. and Mrs. Harold Knapik

85. *Romeo and Juliet*, c. 1948
Oil
20 x 16″
Lent by Cordier & Ekstrom, Inc

86. *Romeo and Juliet*, 1954
Oil
30 x 24″
Lent by Mr. and Mrs. Man Ray

87. *All's Well That Ends Well*, 1948
16 x 20″
Oil
Lent by Mr. and Mrs. Man Ray

*70. *End Game*, 1946
Oil
23¹/₂ x 29¹/₂″
Lent by Dr. and Mrs. Daniel Mattis

71. *Point of View*, 1946
Oil
9¹/₂ x 12″
Lent by Mr. and Mrs. Man Ray

72. *Variation*, 1946, Oil, 14 x 14″
Collection Los Angeles County
Museum of Art, Anonymous Gift

72a. *Untitled*, 1946
Oil
14 x 14″
Collection Los Angeles County
Museum of Art,
Gift of Mrs. Beulah Roth
in Memory of Sanford Roth

73. *The General*, 1947
Oil
16 x 20″
Lent by Mr. and Mrs. Man Ray

*74. *Juliet*, 1947
Oil
24 x 20″
Lent by Mr. and Mrs. Man Ray

75. *Dance in the Subway*, 1948
Oil
17¹/₂ x 23¹/₂″
Lent by Mr. and Mrs. Albert Lewin

*76. *Diamond Cactus*, 1948
Oil
22 x 30″
Lent by Mr. and Mrs. Man Ray

77. *Cafe Man Ray*, 1948
Oil
17³/₈ x 18¹/₄″
Lent Anonymously

58

Infinite Man, 1942
Oil   72 × 50″
Collection of Mr. and Mrs. Man Ray, Paris

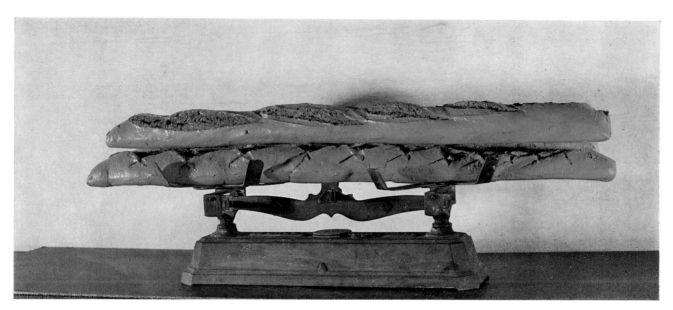

Blue Bread, 1960
Mixed media object   L. 29¹/₂″
Cordier & Ekstrom, Inc., New York

88. *Twelfth Night*, 1948
Oil
33¹/₂ x 29¹/₂″
Lent by Mr. and Mrs. Man Ray

*89. *Macbeth*, 1948
Oil
30 x 24″
Lent by Mr. and Mrs. Man Ray

90. *King Lear*, 1948
Oil
18 x 24″
Lent by Mr. and Mrs. Man Ray

91. *Diderot's Harpsichord
or the Merchant of Venice*, 1948
Oil
36 x 30″
Lent by North Carolina Museum
of Art, Gift of Dr. and Mrs.
Paul Wescher

92. *Aline et Valcour*, 1950
Oil
30 x 38″
Lent by Mr. and Mrs. Man Ray

93. *Comte de Lautréamont*, 1950
Oil
12 x 8¹/₂″
Lent by Mr. and Mrs. Albert Lewin

94. *L'Etoile de Mer*, 1951
Oil
19¹/₂ x 40″
Lent by Leo W. Farland

95. *My First Love*, 1952
Oil
74⁷/₈ x 89″
Lent by Mr. and Mrs. Man Ray

96. *Henriette*, 1952
Oil
72 x 36″
Lent by Mr. and Mrs. Man Ray

*97. *Rue Férou*, 1952
Oil
31¹/₂ x 23¹/₂″
Lent by Samuel Siegler

98. *The Twenty Days and Nights
of Juliet*, 1952
Oil
96 x 120″
Lent by Mr. and Mrs. Man Ray

99. *The P*, 1953
Oil
35 x 58″
Lent by Mr. and Mrs. Man Ray

100. *The New Bridge*, 1954
Oil
Lent by Jacques Kaplan

*101. *Talking Picture*, 1954
Oil with loud speaker
27 x 42″
Lent by Mr. and Mrs. Man Ray

101a. *The Bird of Nowhere*, 1954
Oil
32 x 21¹/₂″
Lent by Mr. and Mrs. Man Ray

*102. *Modern Mythology*, 1955
Oil
57½ x 45"
Lent by Mr. and Mrs. Man Ray

103. *The Harpist*, 1957
Oil
64 x 38"
Lent by Mr. and Mrs. Man Ray

104. *Two-Faced Image*, 1958
Oil
72 x 48"
Lent by Mr. and Mrs. Man Ray

*105. *Peinte Naturelle*, 1958
Oil
14 x 17"
Lent by Mr. and Mrs. Albert Lewin

106. *Piscinema*, 1959
Oil
59 x 47"
Lent by Mr. and Mrs. Man Ray

107. *Without Words*, 1963
Oil
24 x 29
Lent by Mr. and Mrs. Man Ray

PLASTIC PAINTINGS
(series, cat. nos. 108–119)

108. *Untitled*, 1958–65
Oil
16 x 49"
Lent by Mr. and Mrs. Man Ray

109. *Untitled*, 1958–65
Oil
16 x 49"
Lent by Mr. and Mrs. Man Ray

110. *Untitled*, 1958–65
Oil
16 x 49"
Lent by Mr. and Mrs. Man Ray

111. *Untitled*, 1958–65
Oil
16 x 49"
Lent by Mr. and Mrs. Man Ray

112. *Untitled*, 1958–65
Oil
16 x 49"
Lent by Mr. and Mrs. Man Ray

113. *Untitled*, 1958–65
Oil
16 x 49"
Lent by Mr. and Mrs. Man Ray

114. *Untitled*, 1958–65
Oil
19 x 22"
Lent by Mr. and Mrs. Man Ray

115. *Untitled*, 1958–65
Oil
18 x 15"
Lent by Mr. and Mrs. Man Ray

116. *Untitled*, 1958–65
Oil
18 x 15"
Lent by Mr. and Mrs. Man Ray

117. *Untitled*, 1958–65
Oil
18 x 15"
Lent by Mr. and Mrs. Man Ray

118. *Untitled*, 1958–65
Oil
18 x 15"
Lent by Mr. and Mrs. Man Ray

119. *Untitled*, 1958–65
Oil
18 x 15"
Lent by Mr. and Mrs. Man Ray

COLLAGES

120. *Interior*, 1915
Collage
23¾ x 17¼"
Lent by Philadelphia Museum
of Art, A. E. Gallatin Collection

*121. *Theatr*, 1916
Collage
18 x 24"
Lent by Moderna Museet,
Stockholm

REVOLVING DOORS
(series, cat. nos. 122–130)

122. *Long Distance*, 1916–17
Collage
21½ x 13½"
Lent by Galerie Larcade

123. *Orchestra*, 1916–17
Collage
21½ x 13½"
Lent by J. Daniel Weitzman

124. *The Meeting*, 1916–17
Collage
21½ x 13½"
Lent by Richard S. Zeisler

125. *Legend*, 1916–17
Collage
21½ x 13½"
Lent by Galerie Larcade

126. *Decanter*, 1916–17
Collage
21½ x 13½"
Lent by Galerie Larcade

127. *Young Girl*, 1916–17
Collage
21½ x 13½"
Lent by Mrs. Andrew P. Fuller

128. *Shadows*, 1916–17
Collage
21½ x 13½"
Lent by J. Daniel Weitzman

129. *Concrete Mixer*, 1916–17
Collage
21½ x 13½"
Lent by J. Daniel Weitzman

130. *Dragon Fly*, 1916–17
Collage
21½ x 13½"
Lent by J. Daniel Weitzman

*131. *Decollage*, 1917–47
Collage
15½ x 11½"
Lent by Mr. and Mrs. Melvin Jacobs

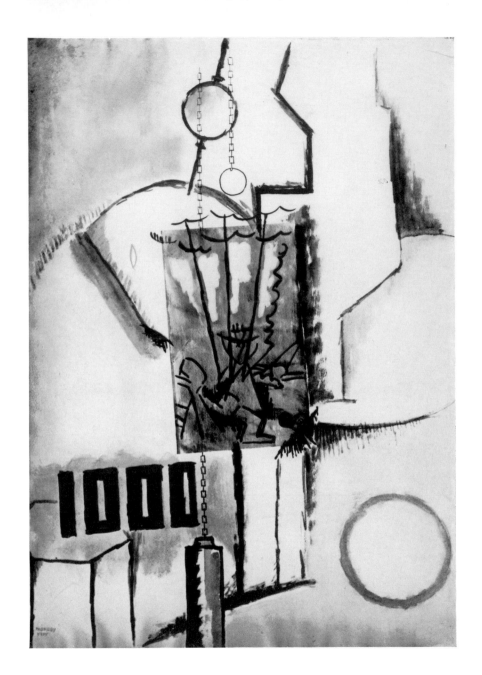

Decoupage, 1915
Oil
(not in exhibition)

132. *Involute*, 1917
Collage
24 x 18″
Lent by Sir Roland and
Lady Penrose

133. *Girls of the Nuts*, 1943
Collage
10 x 17″
Lent by Joseph Hirshhorn

134. *My First Love*, 1952
Collage
19³/₄ x 25″
Lent by Mr. and Mrs. Man Ray

135. *T for Tie*, 1963
Collage
26 x 20″
Lent by Cordier & Ekstrom, Inc.

*136. *Plage Sage*, 1963
Collage
26 x 20″
Lent by Cordier & Ekstrom, Inc.

137. *Light Up Your Gypsies*, 1964
Collage
15 x 18″
Lent by Mr. and Mrs. Man Ray

*138. *Inquietude II*, 1963—65
Collage
26 x 20″
Lent by Mr. and Mrs. Gifford Phillips

139. *Needle and Thread*, 1965
Collage
25³/₈ x 19³/₄″
Lent by The Solomon
R. Guggenheim Museum

*139a. *Serious Man*, 1965
Collage
26 x 20″
Lent by Mr. and Mrs. Raul Alvarez

*139b. *The Necklace*, 1965
Collage
26 x 20″
Lent by Louis F. Kannenstine

SCULPTURE

*140. *By Itself I*,
1966 replica of 1918 original
Bronze
H. 22″
Lent by Galerie Diderot

*141. *By Itself II*,
1966 replica of 1918 original
Bronze
H. 16¹/₂″
Lent by Galerie Diderot

MIXED MEDIA OBJECTS

*142. *Tapestry*, 1911
Mixed media object
65 x 45¹/₂″
Lent by Mr. and Mrs. Man Ray

*143. *Self-Portrait*,
1964 replica of 1916 original
Mixed media object
28 x 19″
Lent by Mr. and Mrs. Man Ray

144. *New York*, 1917,
1966 replica of 1917 original
Mixed media object
H. 19″
Lent by Galerie Diderot

*145. *Lampshade*,
1954 replica of 1919 original
Mixed media object
65 x 25″
Lent by Mr. and Mrs. Man Ray

146. *Puericulture*,
1966 replica of 1920 original
Mixed media object
Lent by Galerie Diderot

147. *Catherine Barometer*, 1920
Mixed media object
47¹/₄ x 11³/₄″
Lent Anonymously

*148. *New York*, 1920,
1962 replica of 1920 original
Mixed media object
11 x 3″
Lent by Mr. and Mrs. Man Ray

*149. *Cadeau*,
1963 replica of 1921 original
Mixed media object
5 x 3¹/₂″
Lent by Mr. and Mrs.
Michael Blankfort

*150. *Indestructible Objects*,
1958 replica of 1923 original
Object to Be Destroyed
Mixed media object
Lent by Mr. and Mrs.
Morton G. Neumann

*151. *Emak Bakia*,
1963 replica of 1927 original
Mixed media object
30⁵/₈ x 11 x 11¹/₈″
Lent by Cordier & Ekstrom, Inc.

*152. *Auto-Mobile*,
1952 replica of 1932 original
Mixed media object
Lent by Galleria Schwarz

*153. *The Orator*, 1935
Mixed media object
39¹/₂ x 58³/₈″
Lent by Galerie Larcade

*154. *Main Ray*, 1935
Mixed media object
Lent by Galleria Schwarz

155. *Palet Table*, 1941
Mixed media object
20 x 37 x 23″
Lent by Mrs. Kate Steinitz

156. *The Silent Harp*, 1943
Mixed media object
24 x 16 x 4″
Lent by I. M. Pei

157. *The Mirage*, 1944
Mixed media object
16 x 8 x 7″
Lent by Leo W. Farland

*158. *Contraption*, 1944
Mixed media object
21 x 8″
Lent by Cordier & Ekstrom, Inc.

*159. *Mr. Knife and Miss Fork*, 1944
Mixed media object
13¹/₂ x 9³/₄″
Lent by Mr. and Mrs. David Savage

*160. *Auto-Portrait*, 1945
Mixed media object
Lent Anonymously

*161. *Optical Hopes and Illusions*, 1946
Mixed media object
21¹/₄ x 7³/₄ x 3⁷/₈″
Lent by Mrs. Patricia Kane Matisse

162. *Obstruction*, 1947
Mixed media object
19 x 22¹/₂ x 6¹/₂″
Lent by Mr. and Mrs. Man Ray

163. *Obstruction*, 1947
Mixed media object
19 x 22¹/₂ x 6¹/₂″
Lent by Mr. and Mrs. Man Ray

*164. *Mirror to Die Laughing By*, 1952
Mixed media object
Lent by Mr. and Mrs.
Morton G. Neumann

*165. *Bookbinding*, 1953
Mixed media object
12 x 10 x 6″
Lent by Frida and Hans Richter

166. *Last Spring*, 1956
Mixed media object
11¹/₂ x 9¹/₂ x 5¹/₂″
Lent by Frida and Hans Richter

*167. *Astrolabe*, 1957
Mixed media object
⌀ 25¹/₂″
Lent by Cordier & Ekstrom, Inc.

168. *Literary Trailer*, 1958
Mixed media object
Lent by Mr. and Mrs. Man Ray

*169. *Smoking Device No. 3*, 1959
Mixed media object
8³/₄ x 9¹/₂″
Lent by Mr. and Mrs. Melvin Jacobs

*170. *Architexture I*, 1960
Mixed media object
Lent by Mr. and Mrs.
Morton G. Neumann

*171. *Blue Bread*, 1960
Mixed media object
L. 29¹/₂″
Lent by Cordier & Ekstrom, Inc.

*172. *It's Springtime*, 1961
Mixed media object
Lent by Mr. and Mrs.
Morton G. Neumann

Enemy Houses, 1933
Oil   39 x 39″
Private Collection

*173. *Person to Person*, 1962
Mixed media object
H. 15³/₄″
Lent by Cordier & Ekstrom, Inc.

174. *Trompe l'Oeuf*, 1963
Mixed media object
21³/₄ x 16″
Lent by Cordier & Ekstrom, Inc.

*175. *Anti-Vol*, 1963
Mixed media object
8¹/₂ x 17″
Lent by Cordier & Ekstrom, Inc.

176. *L'Homme Nouveau*, 1964
Mixed media object
8 x 8 x 16¹/₂″
Lent by Mr. and Mrs.
Frank H. Porter

177. *Red Hot Iron*, 1966
Mixed media object
6 x 3¹/₂″
Lent by Mr. and Mrs. Man Ray

DRAWINGS

178. *Sisters*, 1908
Pencil
21³/₄ x 14¹/₂″
Lent by Mr. and Mrs. David Savage

179. *Stained Glass Window*, 1910
Watercolor, ink
14 x 10³/₄″
Lent by Mr. and Mrs. David Savage

180. *Untitled*, 1913
Watercolor
13³/₄ x 9³/₄″
Lent by P. N. Matisse Gallery

181. *Untitled*, 1914
Ink
19 x 25″
Lent by Mr. and Mrs. Man Ray

182. *Untitled*, 1914
Ink
19 x 25″
Lent by Mr. and Mrs. Man Ray

183. *Untitled*, 1914
Ink
19 x 25″
Lent by Mr. and Mrs. Man Ray

184. *Untitled*, 1914
Ink
19 x 25″
Lent by Mr. and Mrs. Man Ray

185. *Untitled*, 1914
Ink
19 x 25″
Lent by Mr. and Mrs. Man Ray

186. *Untitled*, 1914
Ink
19 x 25″
Lent by Mr. and Mrs. Man Ray

187. *Untitled*, 1914
Ink
19 x 25″
Lent by Mr. and Mrs. Man Ray

188. *Untitled*, 1914
Ink
19 x 25″
Lent by Mr. and Mrs. Man Ray

189. *Untitled*, 1914
Ink
19 x 25″
Lent by Mr. and Mrs. Man Ray

190. *Untitled*, 1914
Ink
19 x 25″
Lent by Mr. and Mrs. Man Ray

191. *Untitled*, 1914
Ink
19 x 25″
Lent by Mr. and Mrs. Man Ray

192. *Untitled*, 1914
Ink
19 x 25″
Lent by Mr. and Mrs. Man Ray

193. *Untitled*, 1914
Ink
19 x 25″
Lent by Mr. and Mrs. Man Ray

194. *Untitled*, 1914
Ink
19 x 25″
Lent by Mr. and Mrs. Man Ray

195. *Untitled*, 1914
Ink
19 x 25″
Lent by Mr. and Mrs. Man Ray

196. *Untitled*, 1914
Ink
19 x 25″
Lent by Mr. and Mrs. Man Ray

197. *Untitled*, 1914
Ink
19 x 25″
Lent by Mr. and Mrs. Man Ray

198. *Untitled*, 1914
Ink
19 x 25″
Lent by Mr. and Mrs. Man Ray

199. *Untitled*, 1914
Ink
19 x 25″
Lent by Mr. and Mrs. Man Ray

200. *Untitled*, 1914
Ink
19 x 25″
Lent by Mr. and Mrs. Man Ray

*201. *Untitled*, 1915
Charcoal
24⁵/₈ x 19″
Lent by The Museum of Modern Art,
Mrs. Donald B. Straus Fund

202. *Black Widow*, 1915
Colored ink
6³/₄ x 4¹/₂″
Lent by Mr. and Mrs. David Savage

203. *Fatigue des Marionettes*, 1919
Watercolor, ink
12⁷/₈ x 14³/₄″
Lent anonymously

204. *Object to Be Destroyed*, 1932
Ink
11¹/₂ x 7³/₄″
Lent by Mr. and Mrs.
Morton G. Neumann

205. *Paranoia*, 1936
Watercolor
13³/₄ x 9³/₄″
Lent by P. N. Matisse Gallery

LES MAINS LIBRES
(for the book of the same title,
cat. nos. 206—226)

206. *Mannikin*, 1940
Ink
18 x 12″
Lent by Princeton University
Art Museum

207. *Untitled*, 1936—37
Ink
25 x 19³/₄″
Lent by Mr. and Mrs. Man Ray

208. *Untitled*, 1936—37
Ink
25 x 19³/₄″
Lent by Mr. and Mrs. Man Ray

209. *Untitled*, 1936—37
Ink
25 x 19³/₄″
Lent by Mr. and Mrs. Man Ray

210. *Untitled*, 1936—37
Ink
25 x 19³/₄″
Lent by Mr. and Mrs. Man Ray

211. *Untitled*, 1936—37
Ink
25 x 19³/₄″
Lent by Mr. and Mrs. Man Ray

212. *Untitled*, 1936—37
Ink
25 x 19³/₄″
Lent by Mr. and Mrs. Man Ray

213. *Untitled*, 1936—37
Ink
25 x 19³/₄″
Lent by Mr. and Mrs. Man Ray

214. *Untitled*, 1936—37
Ink
25 x 19³/₄″
Lent by Mr. and Mrs. Man Ray

215. *Untitled*, 1936—37
Ink
25 x 19³/₄″
Lent by Mr. and Mrs. Man Ray

216. *Untitled*, 1936—37
Ink
25 x 19³/₄″
Lent by Mr. and Mrs. Man Ray

217. *Untitled*, 1936—37
Ink
25 x 19³/₄″
Lent by Mr. and Mrs. Man Ray

218. *Untitled*, 1936—37
Ink
25 x 19³/₄″
Lent by Mr. and Mrs. Man Ray

219. *Untitled*, 1936—37
Ink
25 x 19³/₄″
Lent by Mr. and Mrs. Man Ray

220. *Untitled*, 1936—37
Ink
25 x 19³/₄″
Lent by Mr. and Mrs. Man Ray

221. *Untitled*, 1936—37
Ink
25 x 19³/₄″
Lent by Mr. and Mrs. Man Ray

222. *Untitled*, 1936—37
Ink
11 x 14″
Lent by Mr. and Mrs. David Savage

223. *Untitled*, 1936—37
Ink
11 x 14″
Lent by Mr. and Mrs. David Savage

224. *Untitled*, 1936—37
Ink
11 x 14″
Lent by Mr. and Mrs. David Savage

225. *Untitled*, 1936—37
Ink
11 x 14″
Lent by Mr. and Mrs. David Savage

226. *Untitled*, 1936—37
Ink
11 x 14″
Lent by Mr. and Mrs. David Savage

227. *Shady Rock*, 1938
Ink
11 x 15″
Lent by P. N. Matisse Gallery

228. *Leda and the Swan*, 1940
Watercolor, ink
10 x 13³/₄″
Lent by Mr. and Mrs. David Savage

229. *L'Attente*, 1942
Ink
12 x 14″
Lent by Mr. and Mrs. Vincente Price

230. *Jeu des Visages*, 1950
Watercolor
10 x 14″
Lent by P. N. Matisse Gallery

RAYOGRAPHS

231—248. *Untitled*, 1921—28
(Set of 18 from original
negatives)
Rayographs
Lent by The Museum of
Modern Art

249—285. *Untitled*, 1921—28 (Set of 36)
Rayographs
28 x 19″
Lent by Mr. and Mrs. Man Ray

CHESS SETS

286. *Chess Set*, 1926
Silver
Lent Anonymously

287. *Chess Set*, 1947
Anodized Aluminum
Lent by Michael Asher

*288. *Chess Set*, n.d.
Wood
Lent by Samuel Siegler

289. *Chess Set*, n.d.
Brass
Lent by Leo W. Farland

290. *Chess Set*, n.d.
Wood
Lent by Mr. and Mrs. Man Ray

ORIGINAL EDITIONS

291. *Les Champs délicieux*, 1922
Paris, Société Générale d'Im-
primerie et d'Edition
An album of 12 original photographs
and rayographs with a preface by
Tristan Tzara.
Lent by Mr. and Mrs. Man Ray

292. *Revolving Doors, 1916—17*, 1926
Paris, Editions Surréalistes
Ten color plates in folio. Edition of
105 copies in pouchoir process.
Lent by Mr. and Mrs. Man Ray

293. *Photographies, 1920—34, Paris,* 1934
Published for James Thrall Soby,
Hartford, Connecticut, by Cahiers
d'Art, Paris.
Portrait of Man Ray by Picasso.
Texts by André Breton, Paul Éluard,
Rrose Sélavy (pseudonym of
Marcel Duchamp) and Tristan
Tzara. Preface by Man Ray.
Lent by Mr. and Mrs. Man Ray

294. *Facile*, 1935
Paris, Editions G. L. M.
Poems by Paul Éluard.
Photographs by Man Ray.
Lent by Mr. and Mrs. Man Ray

295. *Les Mains libres*, 1937
Paris, Editions Jeanne Bucher
Poems by Paul Éluard. Drawings
by Man Ray.
Lent by Mr. and Mrs. Man Ray

296. *Les Mains libres*, 1947
Paris, Librairie Gallimard
Half-size reprint.
Lent by Mr. and Mrs. Man Ray

297. *To Be Continued Unnoticed,* 1948
Beverly Hills, Copley Galleries
Lent by Mr. and Mrs. Man Ray

298. *Alphabet for Adults*, 1948
Beverly Hills, Copley Galleries
Drawings
Lent by Mr. and Mrs. Man Ray

299. *Self-Portrait*, 1963
Boston, Atlantic-Little, Brown
American edition.
Lent by Mr. and Mrs. Man Ray

300. *Auto-Portrait*, 1964
Paris, Gallimard
French edition of *Self-Portrait*.
Lent by Mr. and Mrs. Man Ray

The Village,
1913
Oil
20×16″
Collection
Mr. and Mrs.
Albert Lewin,
New York   68

The Rug, 1914
Oil
18$^1/_2$ × 20$^1/_2$″
Collection Mr. and Mrs. Man Ray, Paris

Woman Asleep, 1913
Oil
12×16″
Collection Whitney Museum of American Art,
Gift of Mrs. Katharine Kuh

Man Ray, 1914, 1914
Oil
7 × 5″
Collection Sir Roland
and Lady Penrose,
London

71

Ramapo, 1914
Oil
20 × 19″
Cordier & Ekstrom, Inc., New York

Arrangements of Form, 1915
Oil
17$\frac{1}{2}$ × 11$\frac{1}{2}$″
Cordier & Ekstrom, Inc., New York

Departure of Summer, 1914
Oil   33$\frac{1}{2}$ × 35$\frac{1}{2}$″
P. N. Matisse Gallery, Beverly Hills

Untitled, 1915
Charcoal
24⅝×19″
Collection
The Museum
of Modern Art,
Mrs. Donald B.
Straus Fund

75

Five Figures, 1914
Oil
36 × 32″
Collection Whitney Museum of American Art,
Gift of Mrs. Katharine Kuh

Arrangement of Forms, 1915
Oil
18 × 12″
Collection Mr. and Mrs. Man Ray, Paris

LEGEND

Legend, 1916
Oil
24¹/₄×18¹/₄″
Collection M. and
Mme. Joseph Urvater,
Brussels
(not in exhibition)

78

Love Fingers, 1916
Oil
23⁵/₈×18¹/₈″
Collection E. L. T. Mesens, London
(not in exhibition)

Orchestra, 1916
Oil
52×36″
Private Collection

The Rope Dancer Accompanies Herself with Her
Shadows, 1917
Aerograph
$13^3/_8 \times 17^3/_8''$
Collection Mr. and Mrs. Morton G. Neumann, Chicago

Untitled, 1919
Aerograph
$29^1/_2 \times 23^1/_2''$
Cordier & Ekstrom,
Inc., New York

81

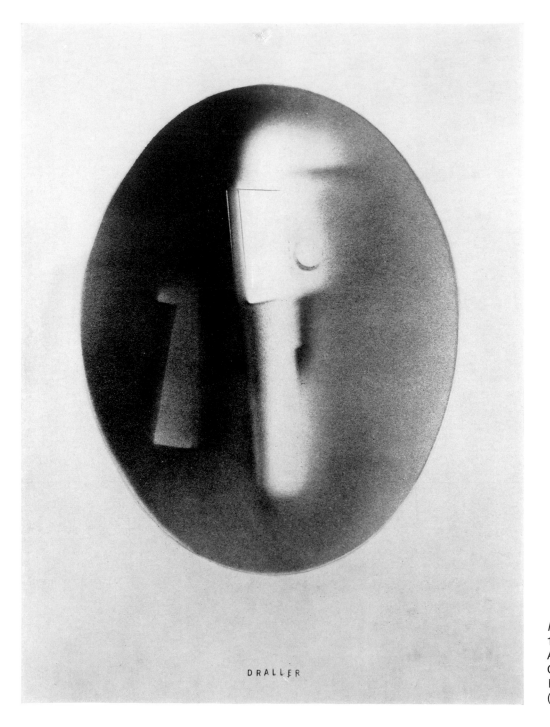

DRALLER

First Object Aerated,
1918
Aerograph
Collection Mr. and
Mrs. Man Ray, Paris
(not in exhibition)

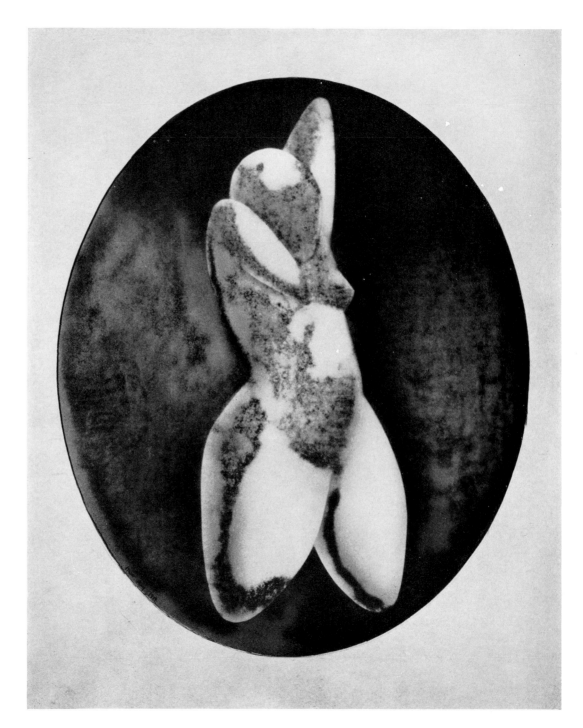

Hermaphrodite,
1919
Aerograph
20×16$^{1}/_{8}$″
Private
Collection

83

Rrose Sélavy,
1923
Oil
23^1/$_4$ × 19^1/$_2$″
Private
Collection   84

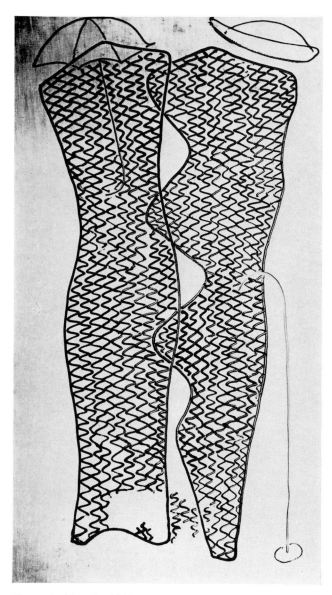

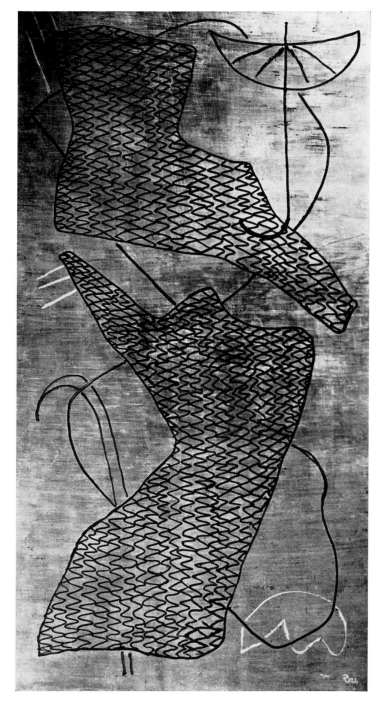

Gens du Monde, 1929
Oil   78³/₄ × 39³/₈"
Collection Mr. and Mrs. Albert Lewin, New York

Gens d'Intérieur, 1929
Oil   78³/₄ × 39³/₈"
Collection Mr. and Mrs. Man Ray, Paris

The Fortune, 1938
Oil
23 × 28″
Collection Mr. and Mrs. Edwin Bergman, Chicago

*The Misunderstood
One*, 1938
Oil
24 × 18″
Collection Mr. and
Mrs. Man Ray, Paris

87

The Wall, 1938
Oil
$19^3/_4 \times 25^1/_2''$
Collection Dr. and Mrs. Howard Taswell,
Rochester, Minnesota

Free Hands, 1936
Drawing
Collection Mr. and Mrs.
Man Ray, Paris

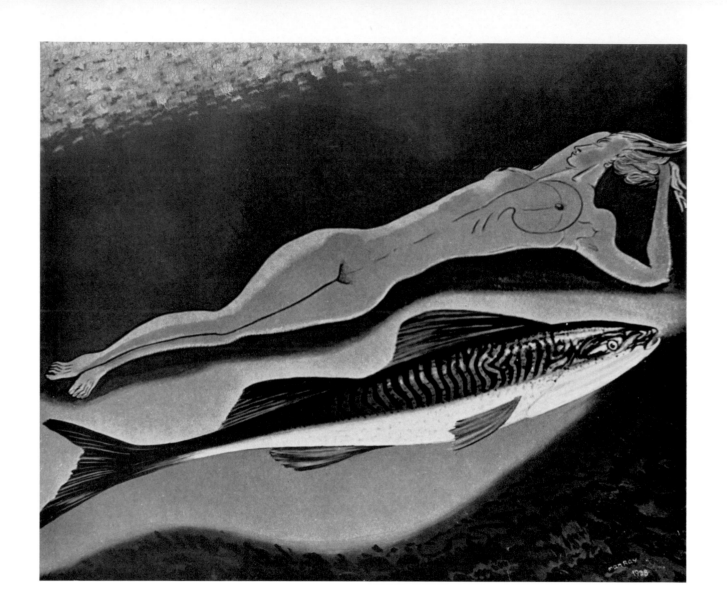

The Woman and Her Fish, 1938
Oil
$23^5/_8 \times 28^3/_4''$
Collection The Tate Gallery, London

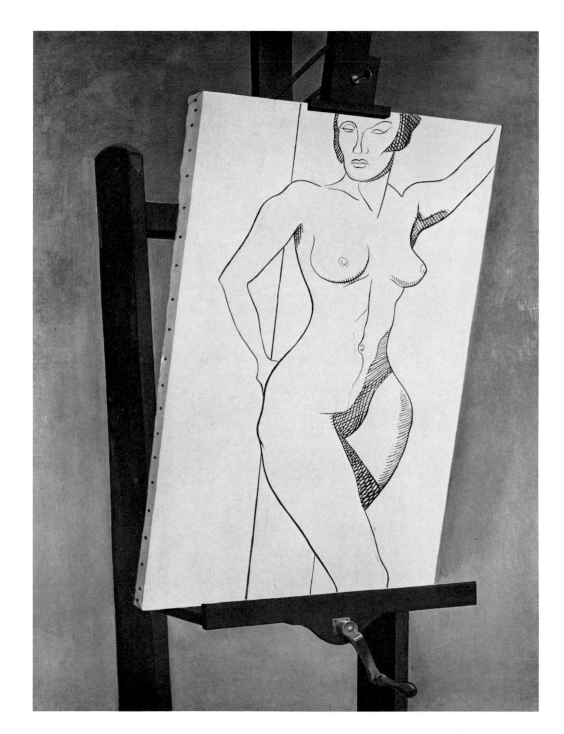

Easel Painting, 1938
Oil
38 × 30″
Collection Mr. and
Mrs. Man Ray, Paris

91

Twins, 1939
Oil
38 × 30″
Collection
Mr. and Mrs.
Man Ray, Paris

92

Abstraction, 1940
Oil
26 x 22″
Collection Los
Angeles County
Museum of Art, Gift
of Dr. and Mrs.
Paul Wescher

93

End Game, 1946
Oil
23¹/₂ × 29¹/₂″
Collection Dr. and Mrs. Daniel Mattis,
Shappaqua, New York

Juliet, 1947
Oil
24 × 20″
Collection Mr. and Mrs. Man Ray, Paris

Diamond Cactus, 1948
Oil
22 × 30″
Collection Mr. and Mrs. Man Ray, Paris

Macbeth, 1948
Oil
30 × 24″
Collection Mr. and Mrs. Man Ray, Paris

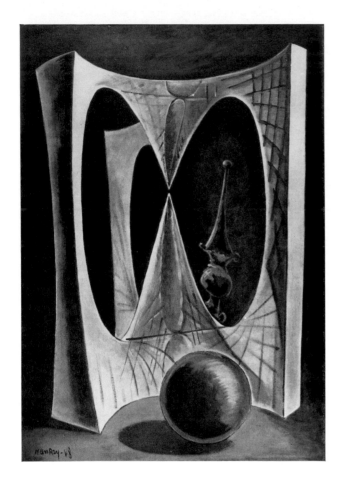

Diderot's Harpsichord or the Merchant of Venice, 1948
Oil
36 × 30″
Collection North Carolina Museum of Art,
Gift of Dr. and Mrs. Paul Wescher

Midsummer Night's Dream, 1948
Oil
25 × 31″
Collection Mr. and Mrs. Herbert Kendall, Princeton,
New Jersey

Rue Férou, 1952
Oil
31¹/₂ × 23¹/₂″
Collection Samuel Siegler, Teaneck, New Jersey

Modern Mythology, 1955
Oil
57¹/₂ × 45″
Collection Mr. and Mrs. Man Ray, Paris

101

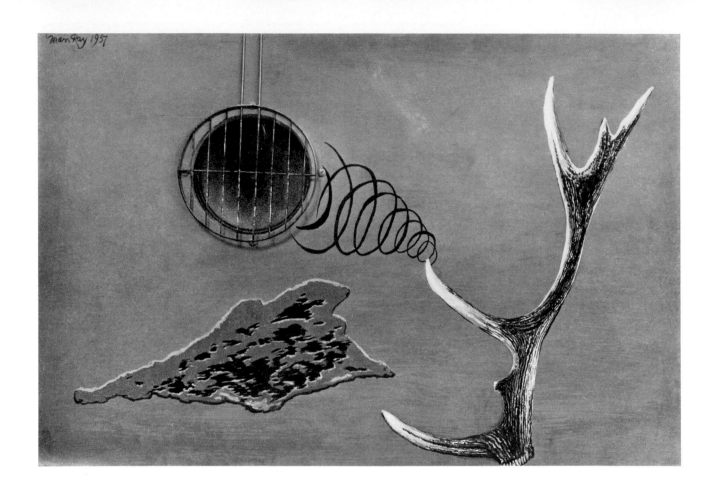

Talking Picture, 1957
Oil with Loud Speaker
27 x 42"
Collection Mr. and Mrs. Man Ray, Paris

Untitled, 1937
Ink
25 x 19³/₄"
Collection Mr. and Mrs. Man Ray, Paris

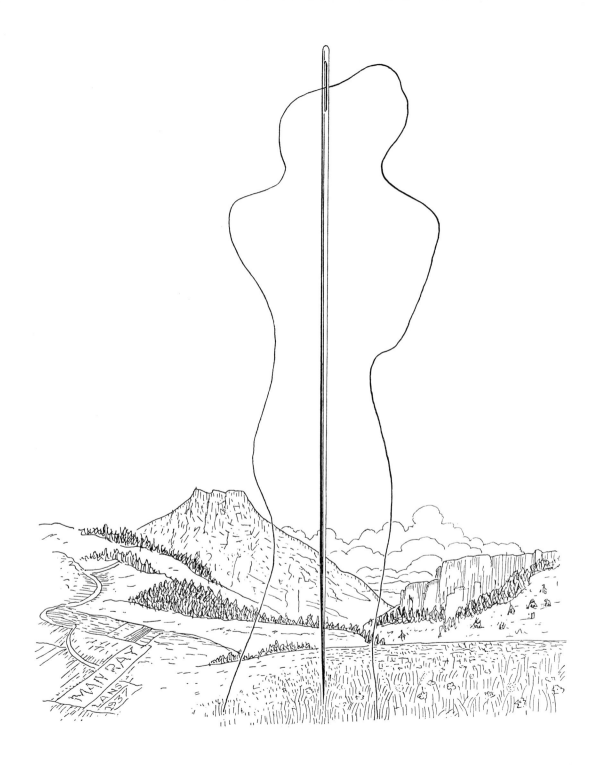

The Turning Point, 1936
Ink drawing
25 × 19³/₄"
Collection Mr. and
Mrs. Man Ray, Paris

Imaginary Portrait of
D. A. F. de Sade, 1936
Ink drawing
25 × 19³/₄"
Collection Mr. and
Mrs. Man Ray, Paris

105

Decollage, 1917—47
Collage
15½ × 11½"
Collection Mr. and
Mrs. Melvin Jacobs,
New York

Decollage, 1944
Collage
Collection Mr. and Mrs. Man Ray, Paris
(not in exhibition)

Plage Sage, 1963
Collage
26 x 20″
Cordier & Ekstrom,
Inc., New York   108

Light Up Your Gypsies, 1964
Collage
15 x 18″
Collection Mr. and Mrs. Man Ray, Paris

Eclipse, 1964
Collage
(not in exhibition)

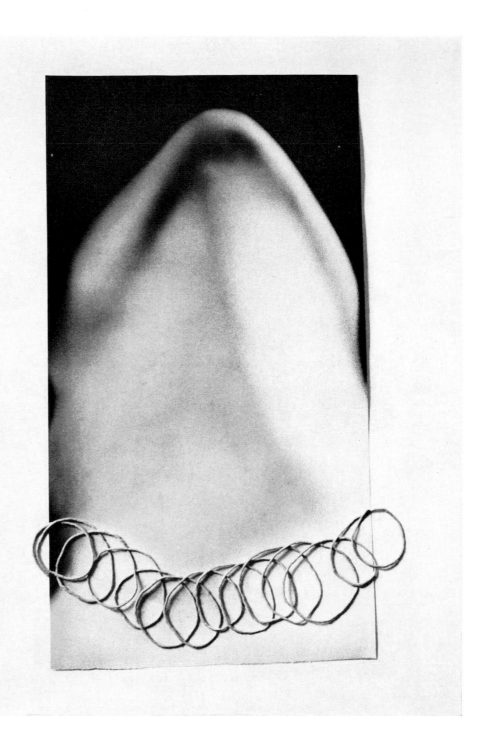

The Necklace, 1965
Collage
26 × 20″
Collection
Louis Kannenstine,
New York

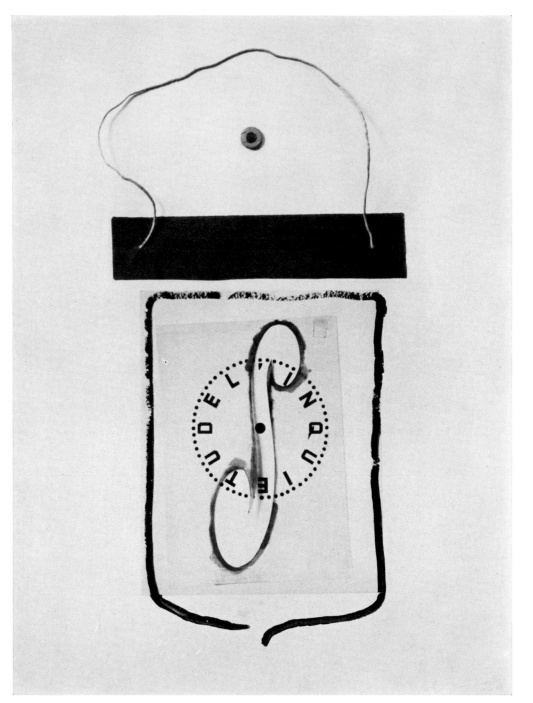

Inquietude II, 1965
Collage
25¹/₂ × 20″
Collection Mr. and
Mrs. Gifford Phillips,
Santa Monica

Untitled, 1965
Collage
113   (not in exhibition)

Serious Man, 1965
Collage
26 × 20″
Collection Mr. and
Mrs. Raul Alvarez,
New York

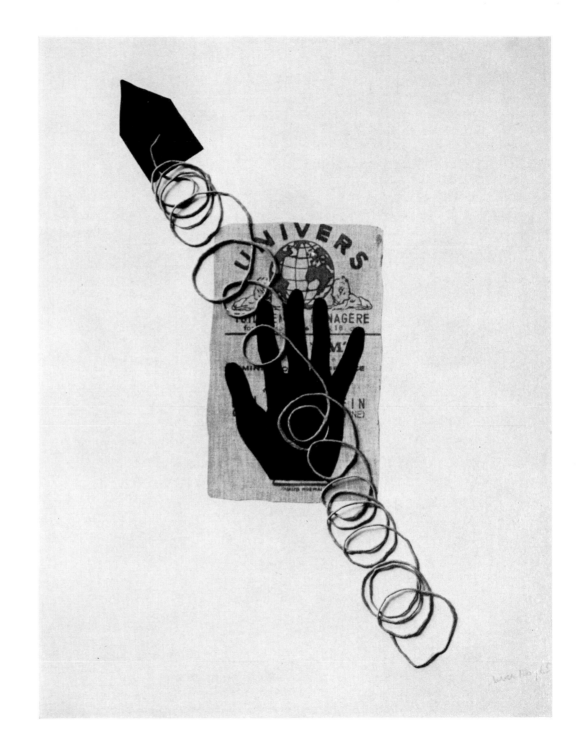

Untitled, 1965
Collage
(not in exhibition)

By Itself I, 1966 replica
of 1918 original
Bronze
H. 22″
Galerie Diderot, Paris

116

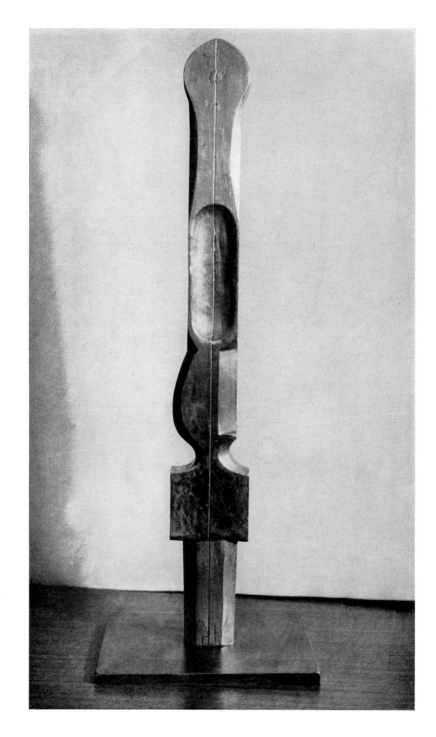

By Itself II, 1966 replica
of 1918 original
Bronze
H. 16¹/₂″
Galerie Diderot, Paris

Lampshade, 1919,
1954 replica of 1919
original
Mixed media object
60 x 25″
Collection Mr. and
Mrs. Man Ray,
Paris

Untitled, 1914
Ink and wash
7^1/$_2$ x 9^1/$_2$"
Collection Los Angeles County Museum of Art,
Gift of Mrs. Florence Homolka

New York, 1920, 1962 replica of 1920 original
Mixed media object
11 × 3″
Collection Mr. and Mrs. Man Ray, Paris

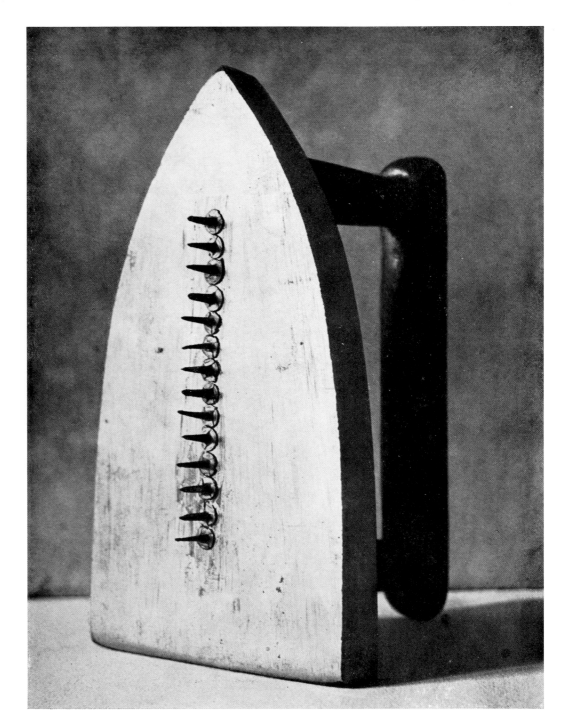

Cadeau, 1921,
1963 replica
of 1921 original
5 × 3$^1/_2$″
Mixed media object
Collection Mr. and
Mrs. Michael Blank-
fort, Los Angeles

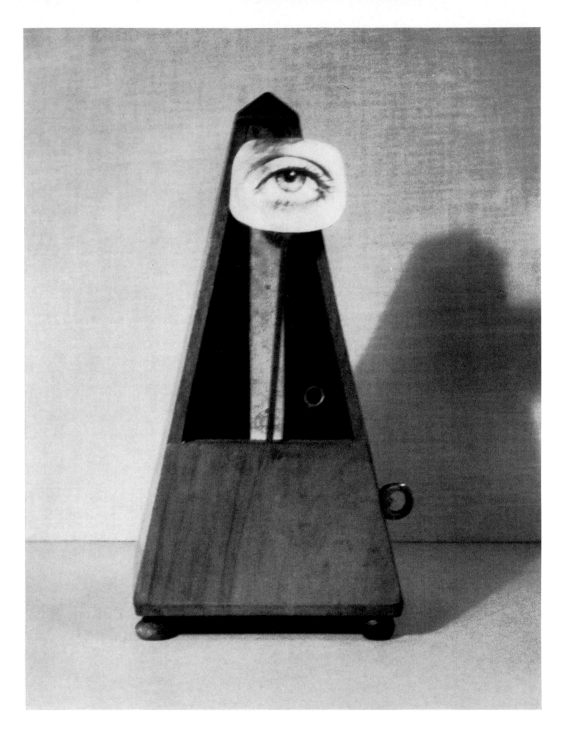

Indestructible Object, 1958 replica of 1923 original *Object to Be Destroyed* Mixed media object Collection Mr. and Mrs. Morton G. Neumann, Chicago

Auto-Mobile, 1932, 1952 replica of 1932 original
Mixed media object
Galleria Schwarz, Milan

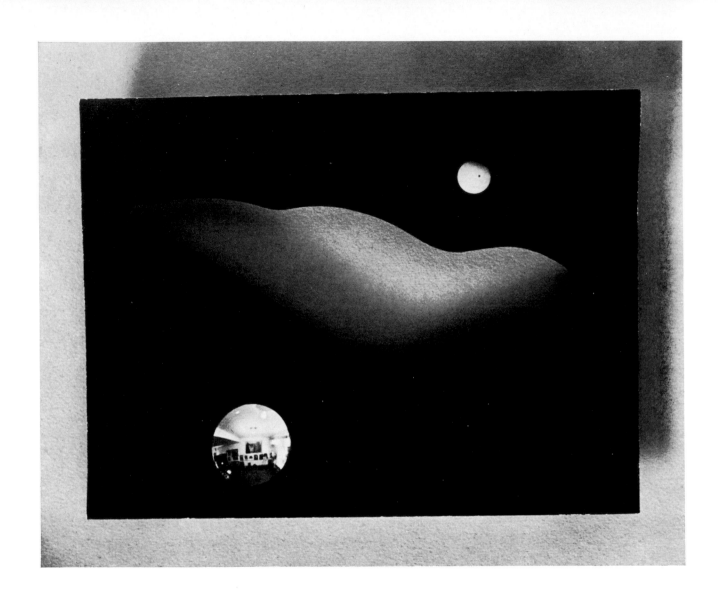

The Orator, 1935
Mixed media object
$39^{1}/_{2} \times 58^{3}/_{4}''$
Galerie Larcade, Paris

The Mirage, 1944
Mixed media object
16 × 8 × 7″
Collection Leo W. Farland,
New York

125

*Optical Hopes
and Illusions*, 1944
Mixed media object
$21^{1}/_{4} \times 7^{3}/_{4} \times 3^{7}/_{8}''$
Collection
Mrs. Patricia Kane
Matisse, New York   126

Contraption, 1944
Mixed media object
21 x 8″
Cordier & Ekstrom, Inc.,
New York

Bookbinding, 1953
Mixed media object
12 × 10 × 6″
Collection Frida
and Hans Richter,
Southbury,
Connecticut

Literary Trailer, 1958
Mixed media object
Collection Mr. and Mrs. Man Ray, Paris

129

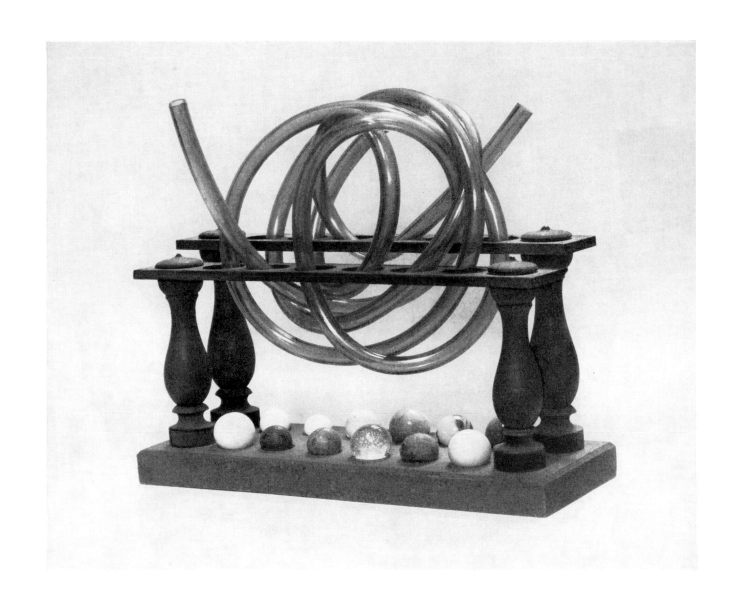

It's Springtime, 1961
Mixed media object
Collection Mr. and Mrs. Morton G. Neumann, Chicago

Smoking Device No. 3, 1959
Mixed media object
$8^3/_4 \times 9^1/_2''$
Collection Mr. and Mrs. Melvin Jacobs, New York

Person to Person, 1962
Mixed media object
H. 15³/₄″
Cordier & Ekstrom,
Inc., New York

Architexture I, 1960
Mixed media object
Collection Mr. and Mrs. Morton G. Neumann, Chicago

133

134

Trompe L'Oeuf, 1963
Mixed media object
$21^3/_4 \times 16''$
Cordier & Ekstrom, Inc., New York

Anti-Vol, 1963
Mixed media object
$8^1/_2 \times 17''$
Cordier & Ekstrom, Inc., New York

135

What We All Lack, 1935,
1963 replica of 1935 original
Mixed media object
Galleria Schwarz, Milan
(not in exhibition)

Astrolabe, 1957
Mixed media object
Ø 25½″
Cordier & Ekstrom, Inc., New York

Main Ray, 1935
Mixed media object
Galleria Schwarz,
Milan   138

Chronology

1890 Born in Philadelphia.

1897 Makes careful crayon copy of the blowing up of the battleship Maine from newspaper pictures. Resolves to become an artist.

1911 First abstraction — of sewing cloth from a fabric book. Titled, *Tapestry*, the work is in the exhibition.

1912 Paints his first "dream" (oneiric) picture. Attends life drawing classes at Ferrer Center in New York.

1913 Marries Adon Lacroix. They move to Ridgefield, New Jersey, where, with the poet, Alfred Kreymborg, they hope to found a community for artists. His wife introduces him to the works of certain French writers, then scarcely known in America, who were to exert an influence upon him — among them, Rimbaud, Lautréamont, Barbey d'Aurevilly.
Attends Armory Show in New York and is influenced in his approach to painting by avant-garde European art in the exhibition.

1915 Returns to New York. First one-man exhibition at Daniel Gallery in New York. Twelve "Fauve-like" sketches bought by the noted collector, A. Jerome Eddy.
Beginning of lifetime friendship with Marcel Duchamp.
Takes up photography.

1916 A founding member of the Society of Independent Artists, Inc., in New York, along with his friends, Duchamp, and the poet and collector, Walter Arensburg.
Participates in the *Forum Exhibition of Modern American Painters* in New York.

1917 Walter Arensberg and H. P. Roche publish the magazines, *The Blind Man* and *Rongwrong*, prompted by Duchamp, Francis Picabia, Jean Crotti and M. R.
First rayographs.

1918 Starts *Aerograph* series, painting with spray gun to achieve soft photographic effects.

1920 With Katherine Dreir, Marcel Duchamp, Henry Hudson and Andrew McLaren founds *Société Anonyme*, the pioneer organization in the United States for the exhibition and collection of modern art. The name, *Société Anonyme*, given by M. R. The collection is at Yale University.

1921 With Marcel Duchamp, edits and publishes the single issue of *New York Dada*.
Goes to Paris where he is welcomed by Parisian Dadaists. First one-man show in Paris at Libraire 6 with catalog notes by Louis Aragon, Paul Éluard, Max Ernst, Georges Ribemont-Dessaignes, Phillipe Soupault and Tristan Tzara.

1922 *Les Champs délicieux*, an album of his photographs, with a preface by Tristan Tzara, is published in Paris.
Participates in *Salon Dada* at Galerie Montaigne in Paris. It is the first international Dada show.

1923 Makes his first film, *Le Retour à la raison*. The print is lost.

1924 Monograph on his work by Georges Ribemont-Dessaignes; titled, *Man Ray*, it is published in Paris.
Appears with Marcel Duchamp, Picabia and Erik Satie in René Clair's film, *Entr'acte*.

1925 Participates in first Surrealist Exhibition at Galerie Pierre in Paris, along with Arp, De Chirico, Ernst, Masson, Miró and Picasso.

1926 A limited edition in color facsimile of the 1916—1917 collage series, *Revolving Doors,* is issued in Paris.
Collaborates with Marcel Duchamp and Marc Allegret in filming of *Anemic Cinema*.
Makes film, *Emak Bakia*.

1928 Makes the film, *L'Étoile de mer*.

1929 Shoots *Les Mystères du Château de dé* at the château of the Vicomte de Noailles.

1932 Participates in *Exposition Retrospective Dada, 1916—1932*, at Galerie de l'Institute, Paris.
In *Surrealist Exhibition* at Julien Levy Gallery, New York, with Dali, Ernst, Picasso and Pierre Roy.

1934 Album of photographs and rayographs from 1920 to 1934, published by James Thrall Soby at Hartford, Connecticut. The volume includes essays and poems by André Breton, Paul Éluard, Rrose Sélavy (Marcel Duchamp), Tristan Tzara and M. R.

1935 *Facile*, a volume of poems by Paul Éluard and photographs by Man Ray, is published in Paris.

1936 Participates in *International Surrealist Exhibition* at New Burlington Gallery, London.
Represented in *Fantastic Art, Dada and Surrealism* exhibition at Museum of Modern Art, New York.

1937 *Les Mains libres*, a book of poems by Paul Éluard and drawings by Man Ray, is published in Paris.
Three Surrealist Painters exhibition at Palais des Beaux-Arts in Brussels. The show presents works by Max Ernst, Yves Tanguy and Man Ray.

1938   Participates in *International Surrealist Exhibition* at Galerie des Beaux-Arts in Paris.

1940   Closes studio in Paris just before Nazi occupation. Flees to Lisbon, carrying no more than valuable lenses and portfolio of his works hurriedly gathered. Arrives in New York and drives cross-country to Hollywood where he takes up residence on Vine Street opposite the "All Night" Ranch Market.

1941   Exhibition of paintings, drawings, rayographs, dated before 1930, at M. H. de Young Museum, San Francisco.

1943   Exhibition of paintings and rayographs at Santa Barbara Museum of Art.

1944   Exhibiion of works in various media from 1913 to 1944 at Pasadena Art Institute.

1945   Exhibition of paintings, drawings, photographs and rayographs at Los Angeles County Museum of History, Science and Art.

1946   Marries Juliet Browner in Beverly Hills in a double wedding ceremony with Max Ernst and Dorothea Tanning.
Exhibition titled, *Objects of My Affection*, at Circle Gallery in Los Angeles.

1948   Exhibition at Copley Galleries, Beverly Hills.
To Be Continued Unnoticed — "Some papers by Man Ray in connection with his exhibition" — is published by Copley Galleries, Beverly Hills.
Alphabet for Adults, a book of drawings, is published by Copley Galleries, Beverly Hills.

1951   Returns to Paris.
Exhibits watercolors at Galerie Berggruen in Paris.

1953   Exhibition of paintings, 1913—1924, at Paul Kantor Gallery, Los Angeles.

1954   Shows *Shakespearean Equations* and other paintings at Galerie Furstenberg, Paris.

1956   Participates in *Three Surrealist Painters* exhibition at Tours Museum with Max Ernst and Dorothea Tanning.

1957   Group of students at exhibition in Paris destroy the metronome in response to title of the work, *Object To Be Destroyed.* M. R. titles new version, *Indestructible Object.*

1958   Represented in *International Dada Exhibition* at Düsseldorf. Contributes statement, *Dadamade,* to catalog.

1959   Exhibition at Institute of Contemporary Art in London.
Participates in *International Surrealist Exhibition* at Galerie Daniel Cordier in Paris.

1960   Drawings and watercolors, 1912—1946, at Esther Robles Gallery, Los Angeles.
Exhibition of photographs at Photokina, Cologne.

Juliet and May Ray in the Studio
Paris
1965
Photograph by René Basset

1961   Awarded Gold Medal at Photography Biennale in Venice.

1962   Exhibition of photographs and rayographs at Bibliothèque Nationale in Paris.

1963   His autobiography, *Self Portrait,* is published in London.
Volume of his photographic *Portraits* is published at Gütersloh, West Germany.
Exhibition of rayographs, 1921—1928 at LGA-Ausstellung in Stuttgart.
Exhibition of paintings, drawings, rayographs, chess sets, books and objects at Princeton University Art Gallery.

1964   Participates in *Le Surréalisme* exhibition at Galerie Charpentier in Paris.
Exhibition of objects, 1920—1964 at Galleria Schwarz in Milan.

1965   Exhibition of objects and collages titled, *Objects of My Affection*, at Cordier & Ekstrom, Inc. in New York.

1966   Participates in *Exposition Dada* at Musée nationale d'Art moderne in Paris.

Major Exhibitions

One-Man Exhibitions

1915 Daniel Gallery, New York. Drawings and paintings.
1916 Daniel Gallery, New York. Drawings and paintings.
1919 Daniel Gallery, New York. Drawings and paintings.
1921 Librairie 6, Paris. 35 works, 1914—1921.
1926 Galerie Surréaliste, Paris. Paintings, objects, rayographs of 1908—1921.
1929 Galerie Quatre Chemins, Paris. Gouaches and rayographs.
Galerie van Leer, Paris. Paintings, early works to 1929.
1932 Galerie Chez Dacharry, Paris. Paintings, 1929—1932.
Julien Levy Gallery, New York. Photographs.
Galerie Vignon, Paris. Recent works.
1934 Lund Humphries and Co., London. Photographs.
1935 Wadsworth Atheneum, Hartford, Conn. Photographs and rayographs.
Art Center School, Los Angeles. Drawings and photographs.
Galeria Adlan, Barcelona. Watercolors and rayographs.
Aux Cahiers d'Art, Paris. Paintings and objects.
1936 Valentine Gallery, New York. Drawings.
1937 Galerie Jeanne Boucher, Paris. Drawings for *Les Mains libres*.

1939 Galerie de Beaune, Paris. Recent Paintings.
1941 M. H. de Young Museum, San Francisco. Paintings, drawings, rayographs before 1930.
Frank Perls Gallery, Los Angeles. Paintings and drawings.
1943 Santa Barbara Museum of Art, Santa Barbara, California. Paintings and rayographs.
1944 Pasadena Art Institute, Pasadena, California. Paintings, drawings, photographs and rayographs, 1913—1944.
1945 Los Angeles County Museum of History, Science and Art. Paintings, drawings, photographs and rayographs, 1913—1945.
Julien Levy Gallery, New York. Paintings and objects.
1946 Circle Gallery, Los Angeles. Objects.
1948 Copley Galleries, Beverly Hills. Watercolors, drawings, objects, photographs, chessmen, books.
1951 Galerie Berggruen, Paris. Watercolors.
1953 Paul Kantor Gallery, Los Angeles. Paintings, 1913—1924.
1954 Galerie Furstenberg, Paris. Shakespearean Equations and other paintings.
1956 L'Etoile Scelle, Paris. Paintings.
1959 Alexander Iolas Gallery, New York. Paintings.
Mayer Gallery, New York. Drawings.
Galerie Larcade, Paris. Paintings, collages, objects, drawings.
Galerie Rive Droite, Paris. Recent paintings.
Institute of Contemporary Art, London. Paintings, drawings, objects, rayographs and photographs, 1908—1959.
1960 Esther Robles Gallery, Los Angeles. Drawings and watercolors, about 1912—1946.
Photokina, Cologne. Photographs.
1962 Bibliotheque Nationale, Paris. Photographs and rayographs. Galerie Rive Droite, Paris. Recent paintings.
1963 LGA-Ausstellung, Stuttgart. Rayographs, 1921—1928.
1963 Cordier & Ekstrom, Inc., New York. Paintings before 1950.
Amiens Museum, Amiens, France. Photographs and rayographs.
Cavendish Gallery, London. Paintings.
Princeton University Art Gallery, Princeton, New Jersey. Paintings, drawings, rayographs, chess sets, books and objects.
1964 Galleria Schwarz, Milan. Objects, 1920—1964.
1965 Cordier & Ekstrom, Inc., New York. Objects and collages.

141

Auto-Portrait, 1944
Object
Mixed media object
Private Collection   142

Seguidilla, 1919
Aerograph
22 x 27¹/₂″
Collection E. L. T. Mesens, London
(not in exhibition)

Selected Group Exhibitions

1916   *Forum Exhibition of Modern American Painters*
       Anderson Galleries, New York.
1917   *Society of Independent Artists Exhibition*
       Grand Central Palace, New York.
1922   *Salon Dada, Exposition Internationale*
       Galerie Montaigne, Paris.
1925   *First Surrealist Exhibition.* Participants include Arp,
       De Chirico, Ernst, Masson, Miró, Picasso and Man Ray.
       Galerie Pierre, Paris.
1926   *Second Surrealist Exhibition.* Same participants as
       year before, with the addition of Duchamp (under the
       pseudonym of Rrose Sélavy and Francis Picabia.

La Galeria Surrealiste, Paris.
International Exhibition of Modern Art, arranged by the Société Anonyme.
Brooklyn Museum of Art, Brooklyn, New York.
1929   *L'Exposition Surréaliste.* Galerie Pierre Colle, Paris.
1930   *Collage.* Works by Arp, Braque, Dali, Duchamp, Ernst,
       Gris, Magritte, Man Ray, Picabia, Picasso, Tanguy.
       Galerie Goemans, Paris.
1932   *Exposition Retrospective Dada, 1916–1932*
       Galerie de l'Institute, Paris.
       Surrealist Exhibition. Works by Dali, Ernst, Picasso,
       Pierre Roy and Man Ray.
       Julien Levy Gallery, New York.
1936   *International Surrealist Exhibition.* Contributions by
       artists from fourteen countries.
       Surrealist Objects. Included African, Pre-Columbian
       and Polynesian art: "found Objects" natural and man-
       made as well as works by the surrealists.
       New Burlington Gallery, London.
       Fantastic Art, Dada, Surrealism
       The Museum of Modern Art, New York.
1937   *Three Surrealist Painters.* René Magritte, Man Ray,
       Yves Tanguy.
       Palais des Beaux-Arts, Brussels.
1938   *Exposition Internationale du Surréalisme*
       Galerie Beaux-Arts, Paris.
       Galerie Robert, Amsterdam.
1947   *Abstract and Surrealist American Art*
       The Art Institute of Chicago.
1948   *Schools of 20th Century Art*
       Modern Institute of Art, Beverly Hills, California.
1951   *Abstract Painting and Sculpture in America*
       The Museum of Modern Art, New York.
1956   *Three Surrealist Painters.* Max Ernst, Man Ray, Doro-
       thea Tanning.
       Musée de Tours, Tours, France.
1958   *Dada*
       Kunstverein für die Rheinlande und Westfalen, Düs-
       seldorf.
1959   *Exposition Internationale du Surréalisme*
       Galerie Daniel Cordier, Paris.
1961   *The Art of Assemblage*
       The Museum of Modern Art, New York.
       Photography Biennale. Venice.
1964   *Le Surréalisme: Sources – Histoire – Affinités*
       Galerie Charpentier, Paris.
1966   *Exposition Dada*
       Musée nationale d'Art moderne, Paris.

Selected Bibliography

By Man Ray

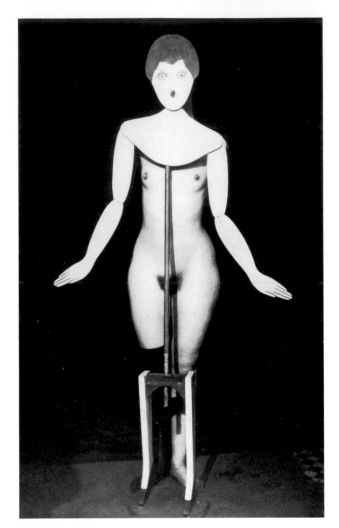

Coat Stand, 1920
Mixed media object
Photograph by Man Ray
(Location unknown)

1915   *A Book of Divers Writings by Adon Lacroix*, designed and published by Man Ray at Ridgefield, New Jersey, 1915.

1921   *New York Dada,* edited by Marcel Duchamp and Man Ray. One issue, April 1921.

1922   *Les Champs délicieux*. Paris, Sociéte Générale d'Imprimerie et d'Édition, 1922. Album de photographies avec une préface de Tristan Tzara. Edition of 40 albums with 12 original photographs and rayographs.

1926   *Revolving Doors, 1916–1917*, Paris, Editions Surréaliste, 1926. Edition of 105 copies in pouchoir process. Ten color plates in folio.

1934   *Photographies, 1920–1934, Paris*, published for James Thrall Soby, Hartford, Connecticut, by Cahiers d'Art, Paris, 1934. Portrait of Man Ray by Picasso. Text by André Breton, Paul Éluard, Rrose Sélavy (pseudonym of Marcel Duchamp) and Tristan Tzara. Preface by Man Ray.

1935   *Facile,* Paris, Editions G. L. M., 1935. Poems by Paul Éluard. Photographs by Man Ray.
"Sur le réalisme photographique," *Cahiers d'Art* [Paris], no. 10, 1935.

1937   *Les Mains libres*, Paris, Editions Jeanne Bucher, 1937. Reprinted (half-size) by Librairie Gallimard, Paris, 1947. Poems by Paul Éluard. Drawings by Man Ray.
La Photographie n'est pas l'art, Paris, Editions G. L. M., 1937.

1941   "Art in Sanity," *Arts and Architecture* [Los Angeles], vol. 58, no. 1, January 1941, pp. 19, 36–37.

1943   "Knud Merrild: A Letter to the Artist from Man Ray," *Arts and Architecture* [Los Angeles], vol. 60, no. 1, January 1943, pp. 27, 46.

1944   *Notes by Man Ray.* Catalog for exhibition at Pasadena Art Institute, 1944.

1945   Statement. Catalog for exhibition at Julien Levy Gallery, New York, 1945.

1948   *To Be Continued Unnoticed,* Beverly Hills, Copley Galleries, 1948. "Some papers by Man Ray in connection with his exposition, December 1948."
Alphabet for Adults, Beverly Hills, Copley Galleries, 1948. Drawings.

"Dadaism," in catalog for *Schools of Twentieth Century Art,* Modern Institute of Art, Beverly Hills, 1948.

1958   "Dadamade," in catalog for exhibition at Kunsthalle, Düsseldorf, 1958.

1959   "An Autobiography," in catalog for exhibition at Institute of Contemporary Art, London, 1959.

"What I Am," [with the help of Erik Satie] in catalog for exhibition at Institute of Contemporary Art, London, 1959. Reprinted in catalog for exhibition at Galleria Schwarz, Milan, 1964.

1963   *Self-Portrait, London,* André Deutsch and Boston, Atlantic-Little, Brown, 1963. French edition, *Auto-Portrait,* Paris, Gallimard, 1964.

Portraits, Güttersloh, West Germany, Sigbert Mohn Verlag, 1963. French edition, Paris, Editions Prisma, 1964. Preface by L. Fritz Gruber. Photographs.

"The Rayograph, 1921–1928," in catalog for exhibition of rayographs at LGA-Ausstellung, Stuttgart, 1963.

About Man Ray

1921   *Exposition Dada: Man Ray,* Paris, Librairie 6, 1921. Notes by Louis Aragon, Paul Éluard, Max Ernst, Georges Ribemont-Dessaignes, Phillipe Soupault and Tristan Tzara.

1922   Tzara, Tristan. "La photographie a l'envers," in *Les Champs délicieux* by Man Ray, 1922.

1924   Ribemont-Dessaignes, Georges. *Man Ray,* Paris, Gallimard, 1924. Re-issued, Peintres Nouveaux, 1937.

1925   Ribemont-Dessaignes, Georges. "Man Ray," *Les Feuilles Libres* [Paris], May–June, 1925.

1929   Desnos, Robert. "The Work of Man Ray," *transition* [Paris], no. 15, 1929.

1934   *Photographies, 1920–1934, Paris,* published for James Thrall Soby, Hartford, Connecticut, by Cahiers d'Art, Paris, 1934. Portrait of Man Ray by Picasso. Texts by André Breton, Paul Éluard, Rrose Sélavy (pseudonym of Marcel Duchamp) and Tristan Tzara. Preface by Man Ray.

1936   Éluard, Paul. "Notes on the Drawings of Man Ray," in catalog for exhibition at Valentine Gallery, New York, 1936.

Levy, Julien. *Surrealism.* New York, Black Sun Press, 1936. With reference to and illustrations by Man Ray and Joseph Cornell.

1944   Clements, Grace. "Art: Los Angeles," *Arts and Architecture* [Los Angeles], vol. 61, no. 10, October 1944, pp. 10, 37.

1945   Riley, Maude. "The Camera Does Lie — Via Man Ray," *Art Digest* [New York], vol. 19, no. 14, April 15, 1945, p. 8.

1949   Millier, Arthur. "Los Angeles Events," *Art Digest* [New York], vol. 23, no. 7, January 1, 1949, p. 17.

The Flat Egg, 1957
Stone
H. 40″
Collection Georges Hugnet, Ile De Rei, France
(not in exhibition)

1953   Wescher, Paul. "Man Ray as Painter," *Magazine of Art* [New York], vol. 46, no. 1, January 1953, pp. 31–37.

Langsner, Jules. "Art News from Los Angeles: Man Ray," *Art News* [New York], vol. 52, no. 2, April 1953, p. 44.

1954 Hulten, Karl G. "Dadaisten Man Ray," *Konstrevy* [Stockholm], April 1954.

1959 Waldberg, Patrick. "Bonjour Monsieur Man Ray!," *Quadrum* [Brussels], no. 7, 1959, pp. 91—102.

Dual Portrait, 1913
Oil
$12^{1}/_{2} \times 10^{1}/_{2}''$
Collection Mr. and Mrs. Man Ray, Paris

Alloway, Lawrence. "Some London Exhibitions: Man Made Objects," *Art International* [Zurich], vol. 3, no. 4—5, 1959, p. 61.

Melville, Robert. "Man Ray in London," *Arts* [New York], vol. 33, no. 9, June 1959, pp. 45—47.

Russell, John. "Art News from London," *Art News* [New York], vol. 61, no. 3, May 1959, pp. 44, 63—64.

1962 Adhemar, Jean. *Man Ray: l'œuvre photographique,* Paris, Bibliotheque Nationale, 1962.

1963 Copley, William. "The Dada of Us All,"*Portfolio* [Art News, New York], no. 7, Winter 1963, pp. 14—23.

Portraits, Güttersloh, West Germany, Sigbert Mohn Verlag, 1963. French edition, Paris. Editions Prisma, 1964. Preface by L. Fritz Gruber. Photographs.

Goldwater, Robert. "An Exciting Ride in the Van," *Saturday Review* [New York], vol. 46, no. 30, August 17, 1963, p. 19.

O'Doherty, Brian. "Man Ray: Prophet of Art," *New York Times*, May 3, 1963, p. 37.

O'Doherty, Brian. "Light on an Individual: Man Ray," *New York Times,* May 5, 1963, Part II, p. 15.

1964 Belz, Carl I. "Man Ray and New York Dada," *The Art Journal* [New York], vol. 23, no. 3, Spring 1964, pp. 207—213.

Marder, Irving. "Man Ray: On Dada and Pop Art," *New York Times* [International Edition, Paris], February 6, 1964.

Kelleher, Patrick. Statement. Catalog for exhibition at Princeton University Art Gallery, 1964.

Belz, Carl I. Statement. Catalog for exhibition at Princeton University Art Gallery, 1964.

Barnet, Ed Willis. "What a Man Ray!," *PSA Journal* [official publication of the Photographic Society of America], November 1964.

1965 Belz, Carl I. "The Film Poetry of Man Ray," *Criticism* [Wayne State University Press, Detroit], Spring 1965, pp. 117—130.

General Works

1928 Breton, André. *Le surréalisme et la peinture,* Paris, Editions N. R. F., 1928, revised edition, Paris, Gallimard, 1963.

1931 Ribemond-Dessaignes, Georges. "Histoire de dada," *La Nouvelle Revue Française* [Paris], no. 36, 1931.

1932 *This Quarter* [Paris], September 1932. Surrealist number edited by André Breton.

Hugnet, Georges. *L'Esprit dada dans la peinture,* Paris, Cahiers d'Art, 1932.

1934 Read, Herbert. *Art Now*, London, Faber and Faber, 1934. Reprinted by Pitman Publishing Company, New York, Toronto, London, 1948.

1935 *Cahiers d'Art* [Paris], no. 5—6, 1935. Surrealist number edited by Christian Zervos.

Hughe, René. *Histoire de l'art contemporaine,* Paris, Alcan, 1935.

1936 Barr, Alfred H. Jr., editor. *Fantastic Art, Dada, Surrealism,* New York, The Museum of Modern Art, 1936. Includes two essays by Georges Hugnet: "Dada" and "In the Light of Surrealism."
Gascoyne, David. *A Short Survey of Surrealism,* London, Cobden-Sanderson, 1936.
Minotaur [A. Skira, Paris], June 15, 1936. Surrealist issue edited by E. Teriade.
Breton, André. "What is Surrealism?," *Criterion Miscellany, No. 43,* London, Faber and Faber. Reprinted in *Paths to the Present,* edited by Eugen Weber, Dodd, Mead and Company, New York, 1960.
Cahiers d'Art [Paris], no. 1–2, 1936. Surrealist number edited by Christian Zervos.
1938 Zervos, Christian. *Histoire de l'art contemporaine,* Paris, Cahiers d'Art, 1938.
1942 Guggenheim, Peggy, editor. *Art of This Century,* New York, Art of This Century Gallery, 1942. "An anthology of non-realistic art covering the period from 1910 to 1942."
1948 Peyre, Henri. "The Significance of Surrealism," *Yale French Studies,* New Haven, Connecticut, Yale University, Fall—Winter, 1948.
Barr, Alfred H. Jr., *Painting and Sculpture in the Museum of Modern Art,* New York, The Museum of Modern Art, 1948.
1949 San Lazzaro, G. Di. *Painting in France, 1895–1949,* New York, Philosophical Library, 1949.
1950 Hamilton, George Heard, editor. *Collection of the Société Anonyme,* New Haven, Connecticut, Yale University Art Gallery, 1950.
1951 Motherwell, Robert, editor. *The Dada Painters and Poets,* New York, Wittenborn, Schultz, Inc., 1951. Includes contributions from the period by Arthur Craven, Gabrielle Buffet-Picabia, Erik Satie, Richard Huelsenbeck, Hugo Ball, Kurt Schwitters, Jacques Vaché, Tristan Tzara, Georges Ribemont-Dessaignes, Georges Hugnet, André Breton, Jean Arp, Paul Éluard, Hans Richter, Albert Gleizes, Raoul Hausmann, and an exhaustive bibliography by Bernard Karpel.
Baur, John I. H. *Revolution and Tradition in Modern American Art,* Cambridge, Massachusetts, Harvard University Press, 1951.
Ritchie, Andrew C. *Abstract Painting and Sculpture in America,* New York, The Museum of Modern Art, 1951.
1952 Connolly, Cyril. "Surrealism," *Art News Annual, XXI* [New York], vol. 50, no. 7, 1952, pp. 131–162, 164, 166, 168, 170.
1953 Read Herbert. *The Philosophy of Modern Art,* New York, Horizon Press, 1953. Reprinted by Meridian Books, New York, 1955.

Emak Bakia, 1963 replica of 1927 original
Mixed media object
$30^{5}/_{8} \times 11 \times 11^{1}/_{8}''$
Cordier & Ekstrom, Inc., New York

1954 Barr, Alfred H. Jr., editor. *Masters of Modern Art,* New York, The Museum of Modern Art, 1954.

1955 Brown, Milton W. *American Painting from the Armory Show to the Depression,* Princeton, New Jersey, Princeton University Press, 1955.

1956 Blesh, Rudi. *Modern Art USA: Men, Rebellion, Conquest, 1900—1956,* New York, Alfred Knopf, 1956.

1957 Seuphor, Michel. *Dictionary of Abstract Painting,* New York, Tudor Publishing Company, 1957.
Verkauf, Willy, editor. *Dada: Monograph of a Movement,* New York, George Wittenborn, Inc., 1957.

1958 Nadeau, Maurice. *Histoire du Surréalisme,* Paris, Editions du Seuil, 1958.

1959 Jean, Marcel. *The History of Surrealist Painting,* Paris, Editions du Seuil, 1959, New York, Grove Press, 1960.
Balakian, Anna. *Surrealism: the road to the absolute,* New York, Noonday Press, 1959.

1961 Seitz, William. *The Art of Assemblage,* New York, The Museum of Modern Art, 1961.

1962 Janis, Harriet and Rudi Blesh. *Collage: Personalities, Concepts Techniques*, Philadelphia, New York, Chilton Company, 1962.
Waldberg, Patrick. *Surrealism,* Lausanne, Editions d'Art Abert Skira, 1962. Distributed in the United States by World Publishing Company, Cleveland.

1964 Newhall, Beaumont. *The History of Photography,* New York, The Museum of Modern Art, 1964.
Le Surréalisme: Sources — Histoire — Affinités. Catalog for exhibition at Galerie Charpentier, Paris, 1964.

1966 Richter, Hans. *Dada: Art and Anti-Art*, New York, Toronto, McGraw-Hill Book Company, 1966.

Man Ray
Cadaques, Spain
1963
Photograph by Mrs. Man Ray

Library of Congress Catalog Number 66-29095
Printed in Western Germany by Brüder Hartmann, Berlin